Irvin H. Mack, J. Lincoln Hall

Boundless Love

a book of songs prepared for use in Sunday schools, evangelistic services and young peoples' meetings

Irvin H. Mack, J. Lincoln Hall

Boundless Love

a book of songs prepared for use in Sunday schools, evangelistic services and young peoples' meetings

ISBN/EAN: 9783337264611

Printed in Europe, USA, Canada, Australia, Japan

Cover: Foto ©Lupo / pixelio.de

More available books at **www.hansebooks.com**

Boundless Love

A Book of Songs prepared for use in

SUNDAY SCHOOLS

EVANGELISTIC SERVICES

....and....

YOUNG PEOPLES' MEETINGS

...By...

J. LINCOLN HALL and IRVIN H. MACK

PHILADELPHIA:	NEW YORK:
HALL=MACK CO.	WARD & DRUMMOND
PUBLISHERS	PUBLISHERS
416 Arch Street	164 Fifth Avenue

Preface.

BOUNDLESS LOVE is placed before the thousands of Christian worshipers, by its authors, with merely the statement, that they trust the songs, within its pages, may help in the service of God, and in the praise of the Lord, Jesus Christ.

The success of the various efforts of these authors, and the numerous inquiries for a book, have led them to the preparation of Boundless Love.

Great care has been exercised to secure compositions that are particularly adapted to use in Sunday Schools, Evangelistic Services and Young Peoples' Meetings.

J. LINCOLN HALL,
IRVIN H. MACK.

BOUNDLESS LOVE. Concluded.

Sent to sin-ners poor and low-ly, Sent to make them pure and ho-ly,

D.S.

Bound-less, bound-less love, From Thy throne a-bove,

LISTEN! LISTEN! HE IS CALLING.

J. Q.
JOSEPHINE QUERNS.

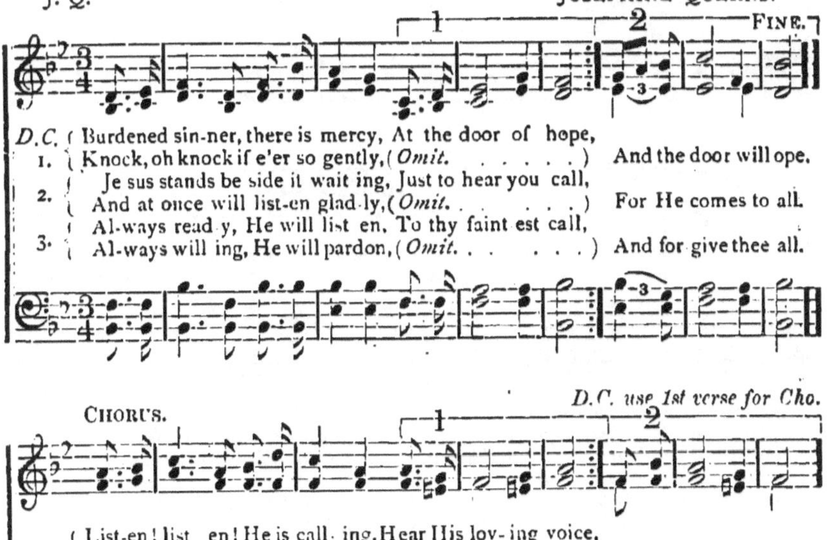

D.C.
1. { Burdened sin-ner, there is mercy, At the door of hope,
   { Knock, oh knock if e'er so gently, (*Omit*. . . . . .) And the door will ope.
2. { Je sus stands be side it wait ing, Just to hear you call,
   { And at once will list-en glad-ly, (*Omit*. . . . . .) For He comes to all.
3. { Al-ways read y, He will list en, To thy faint est call,
   { Al-ways will ing, He will pardon, (*Omit*. . . . . .) And for give thee all.

CHORUS.   D.C. *use 1st verse for Cho.*

{ List-en! list en! He is call-ing, Hear His lov-ing voice,
{ Hear His spir-it gent ly pleading, (*Omit*. . . . . .) Make Him now your choice.

Copyright, 1896, by Hall-Mack Co.

3 We march—where saintly heroes,
  Have won their best renown,
  And sword and flame their faith o'ercame,
  To gain their martyr's crown.
  ‖: Alleluia ! Alleluia !
  God will never fail His own. :‖

4 We march—where the sweet music,
  Of angels cheer us on,
  Who guard our way by night and day,
  Till all our foes are gone.
  ‖: Alleluia ! Alleluia !
  God has our redemption won. :‖

5 We march—where Jesus calls us
  To Zion's radiant dome;
  And soon or late within the gate,
  His ransomed all will come.
  ‖: Alleluia ! Alleluia !
  God will bring the children home. :‖

6 We march—in hope rejoicing,
  The war will soon be done, [bring,
  And Christ, our King, the world will
  To bow before His throne.
  ‖: Alleluia ! Alleluia !
  God shall reign, and God alone. :‖

Copyright, 1895, by Hall-Mack Co.

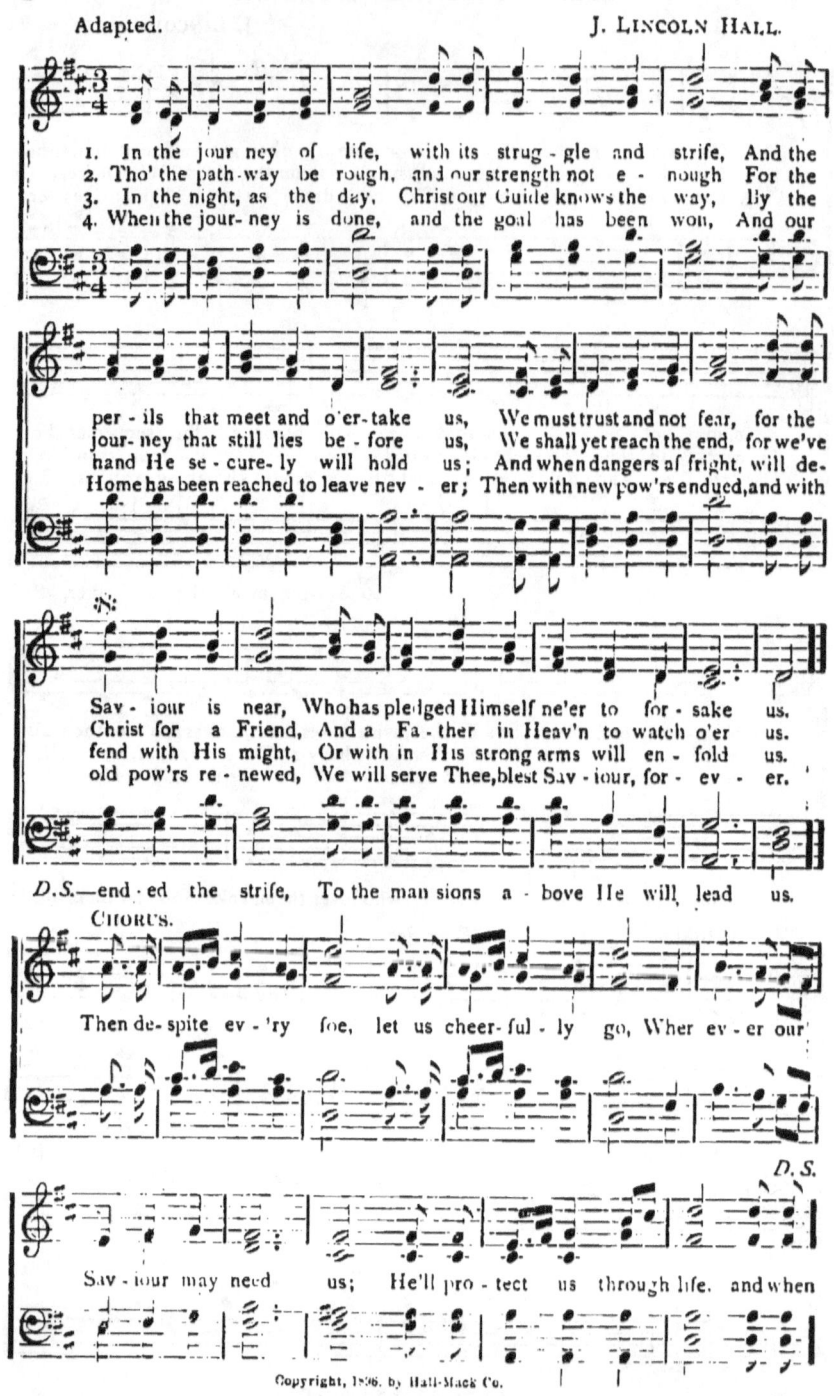

CARRY THE MESSAGE. Concluded.

car - ry the mes - sage, car- ry the wonderful mes - sage, The mes- sage of heav- en - ly love.

SWEET MOMENTS.

IRVIN H. MACK. HOWARD CLARE.

1. Sweet mo-ments when we feel, The Sav-iour's pres-ence near,
   When bless-ings o'er us steal, His lov-ing voice we hear.
2. O won-der-ful the peace, O mo-ments ev-er sweet,
   What bless-ings on us fall. When-e'er the Lord we meet.
3. Let fleet-ing mo-ments, Lord, Be turned to hours of praise;
   With hearts and arms of strength, Thy ban-ner we shall raise.

CHORUS.

Sweet are the mo - ments When-e're the bless- ings fall;
Glad is the heart When Christ is all in all.

Copyright, 1895, by Hall-Mack Co.

O FOR A NOBLER, BRIGHTER LIFE.

IRVIN H. MACK. HOWARD CLARE.

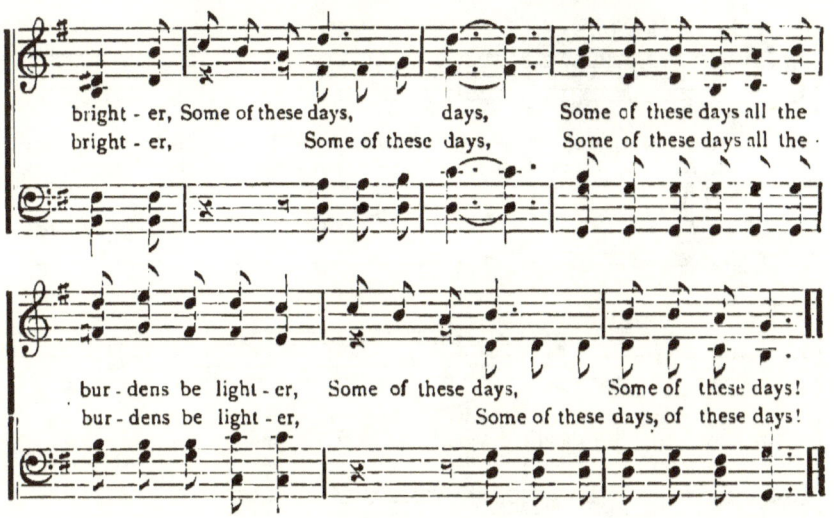

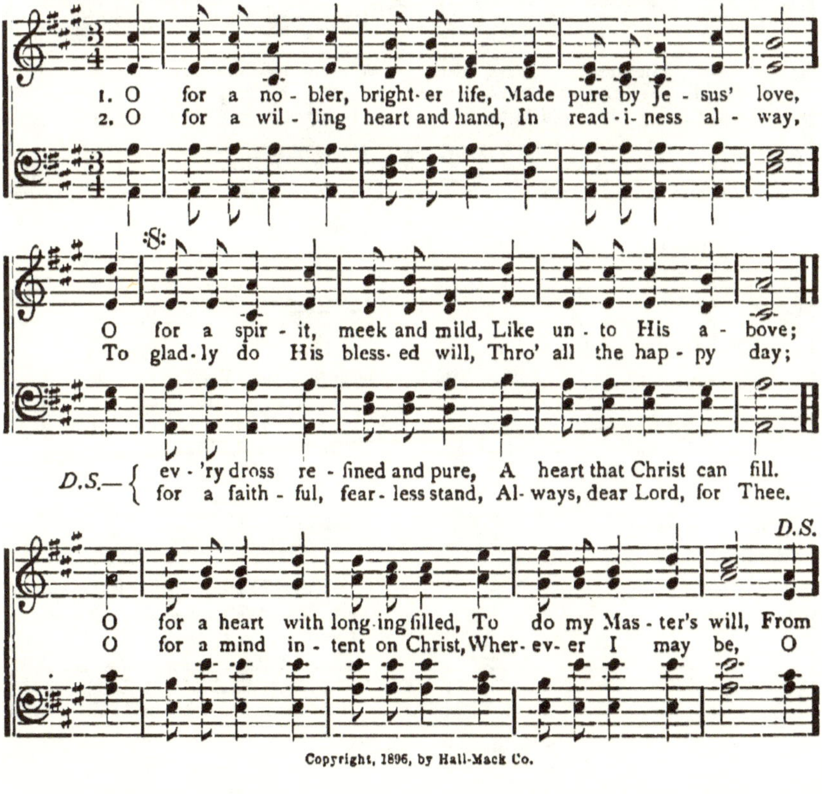

Walking by the Saviour's Side. Concluded.

walk - ing,
walk-ing with Je - sus, Walk-ing where no harm can e'er be - tide.

BLESSED SAVIOUR, LEAD US.

EMILY P. MILLER. J. LINCOLN HALL.

1. Just to let the Sav-iour Lead us where He will, Tho' 'tis through the
2. Ev-er trust-ing Je-sus, Glad to do His will, E'en tho' thorns and
3. Nev-er shirk-ing du-ty, Tho' we're sore-ly pressed, Know-ing that He

des-ert, Or by moss-y rill.
bri-ars Make the good seem ill.
work-eth, All things for the best.

CHORUS.

Bless-ed Sav-iour, lead us,
Bless-ed Sav-iour, lead us, lead us,
Dai-ly by the hand, Then we'll safely jour-ney To the promised land.

Copyright, 1895, by Hall-Mack Co.

REDEMPTION. Concluded.

Saved, O yes, I'm saved; Thro' Jesus' blood and righteousness, I now am saved.

GLORY TO THE CLEANSING BLOOD.

VERA. J. LINCOLN HALL.

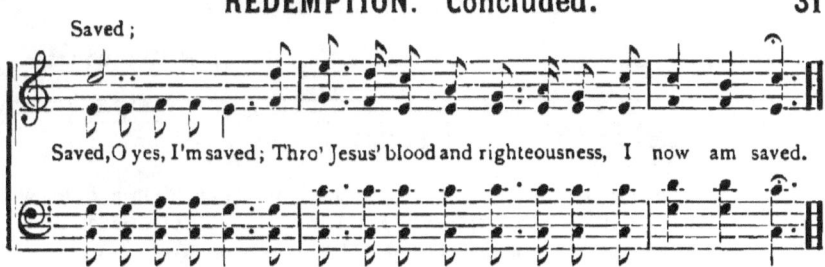

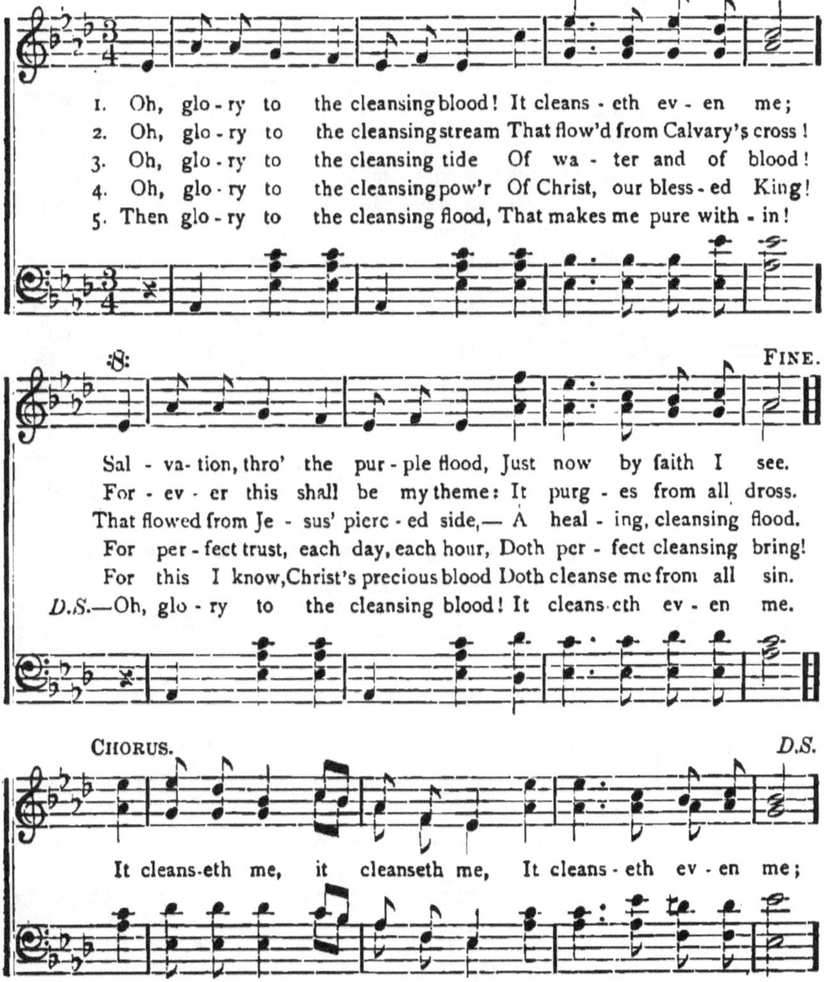

1. Oh, glo-ry to the cleansing blood! It cleans-eth ev-en me;
2. Oh, glo-ry to the cleansing stream That flow'd from Calvary's cross!
3. Oh, glo-ry to the cleansing tide Of wa-ter and of blood!
4. Oh, glo-ry to the cleansing pow'r Of Christ, our bless-ed King!
5. Then glo-ry to the cleansing flood, That makes me pure with-in!

Sal-va-tion, thro' the pur-ple flood, Just now by faith I see.
For-ev-er this shall be my theme: It purg-es from all dross.
That flowed from Je-sus' pierc-ed side,— A heal-ing, cleansing flood.
For per-fect trust, each day, each hour, Doth per-fect cleansing bring!
For this I know, Christ's precious blood Doth cleanse me from all sin.

D.S.—Oh, glo-ry to the cleansing blood! It cleans-eth ev-en me.

CHORUS. D.S.

It cleans-eth me, it cleanseth me, It cleans-eth ev-en me;

Copyright, 1896, by Hall-Mack Co.

38. WORK FOR ALL TO DO.

Selected.   J. Lincoln Hall.

1. O! this world is in-tend-ed for work-ing, Not for wish-ing, but push-ing a-long; . . . And our du-ty we would not be shirk-ing, . . . Yet we'll light-en our la-bor with song. . . .
2. There are plen-ty of wrongs to be right-ed, Ma-ny foul things want sweep-ing a-way, . . . Ma-ny dark plac-es need to be light-ed, . . . And the time to be-gin is to-day. . . .
3. O! this world is in-tend-ed for glad-ness, Not for pov-er-ty, suff-'ring and wrong, . . . Let us root out the caus-es of sad-ness, . . . Un-til weep-ing is changed in-to song. . . .
4. Let us press t'wards the goal of the Mas-ter,— A world that's un-self-ish and kind; . . . Would to God we were all mov-ing fast-er, . . . And that none were found lag-ging be-hind. . . .

Copyright, 1896, by Hall-Mack Co.

SOUNDING HIS PRAISES. Concluded.

JESUS IS CALLING THE CHILDREN.

HOWARD CLARE.

Copyright, 1895, by Hall-Mack Co.

42. DRIFTING.

Irvin H. Mack. — J. Lincoln Hall.

1. Drift-ing, drifting with the cur-rent, Toss'd by wind and swept by tide, Down-ward, downward sweeps the wa-ter, Sweeps the current's treach'rous glide.

2. Broth-er, whither are you drift-ing? See the rapids just a-head? Haste thee, quick-ly turn to ref-uge, Let thy life by Christ be led. List-en, list-en, hear the thun-ders, Haste thee, brother, turn to Je-sus.

Copyright, 1896, by Hall-Mack Co.

BEAUTIFUL HOME.

IRVIN H. MACK. FRANK L. ARMSTRONG.

1. Let us sing the sweet song of that beau-ti-ful home, Of the home far a-way with the Mas-ter; Where no storms ere as-sail, where no tempests pre-vail, And no per-ils bring grief and dis-as-ter.
2. There my soul in that home with the ransomed shall dwell, In un-chang-a-ble love ere a-bid-ing; There to shine like the stars in their bril-lian-cy bright, In the bos-om of Christ be re-sid-ing.
3. O this home is for all who will serve the dear Lord, Sin-ner, come to Him now all con-fess-ing; O how sweet is the rest of the hap-py and blest, And to all who His love are pos-sess-ing.

CHORUS.

Far a-way from this vale 'midst the an-gels a-bove, With the saints of the Lord to be sing-ing; I shall rest with the Lord, there to

Copyright, 1896, by Hall-Mack Co.

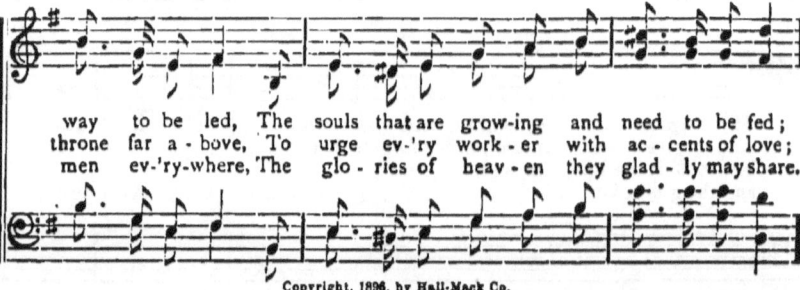

TO WORK, TO WORK! Concluded. - 51

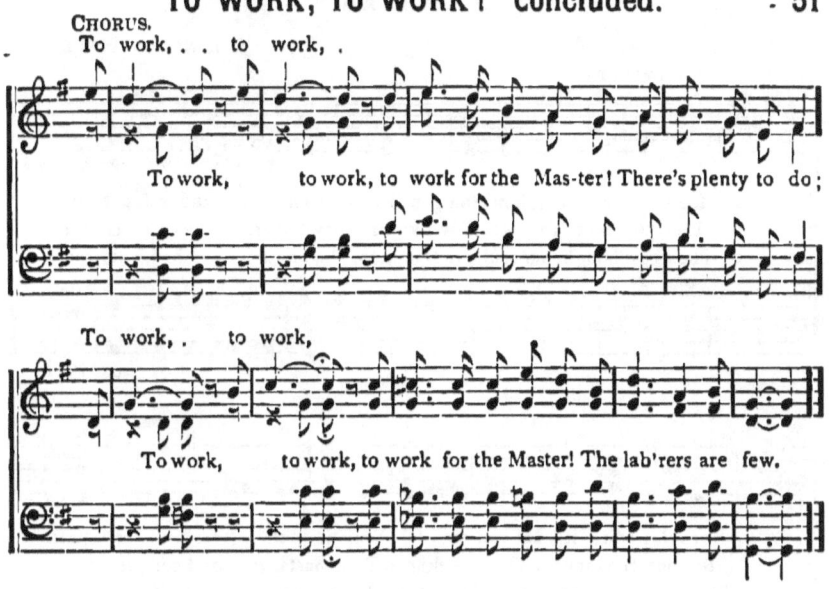

FOREVER I'LL BE THINE.

C. B. CHARLES BENTLEY.

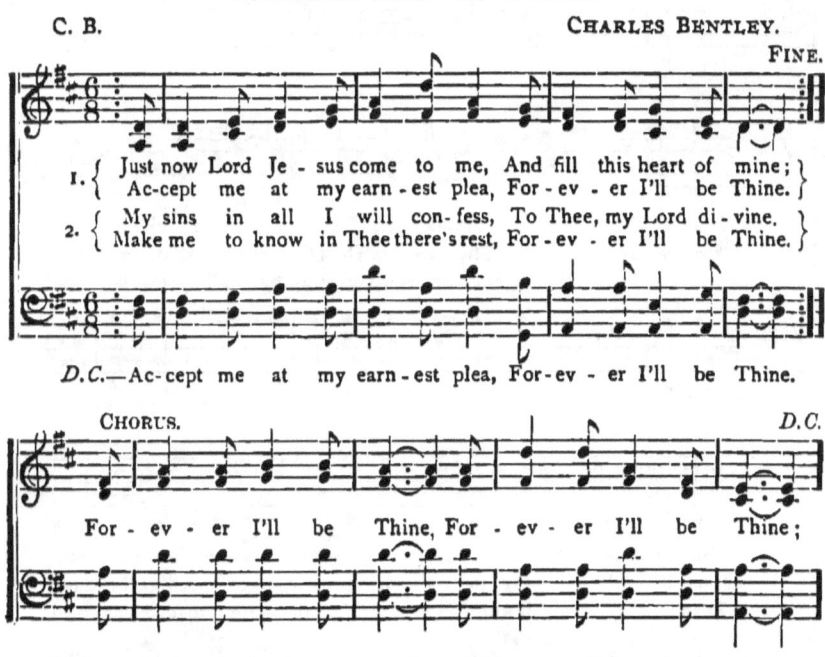

3 Help me to shun my passions great,
   That tempt me on this line;
 Lest I should be forever late
   To be forever Thine.

4 Thy grace will keep me on my way,
   I all to Thee resign;
 For Thou wilt keep me day by day,
   Forever I'll be Thine.

Copyright, 1896, by Charles Bentley.

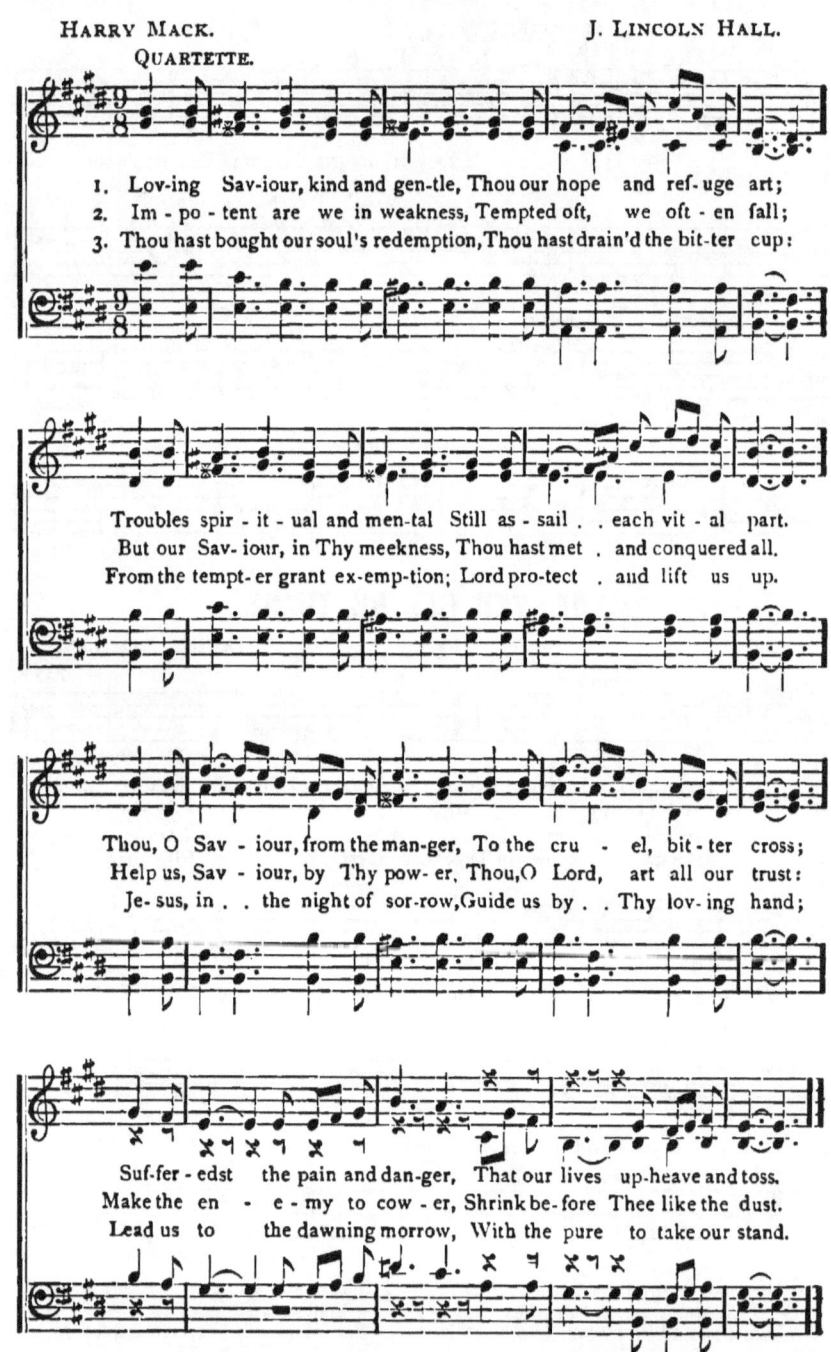

CHRIST IS THE CONQUEROR. Concluded.

O glo-ri-ous con-quer-or, Who leads to vic-to-ry.

LAMBS OF JESUS.

EMILY P. MILLER. J. LINCOLN HALL.

1. We are lambs of Je - sus, In His fold we'll stay,
2. How He watch es o'er us, With such love and care,
3. He's a faith- ful Shep - herd, Al - ways kind and true,
4. And this lov - ing Shep - herd, Grieves if we are sad,

For our lov - ing Shep - herd, Guards us, lest we'd stray.
Guid' - ing lit - tle foot - steps In - to paths so fair.
Pa - tient and for - giv - ing, Ma - ny faults or few.
But with us re - joic - es, When He makes us glad.

CHORUS.

We are lambs of Je - sus, E - vil we'll not fear,

For our lov - ing Shep - herd, Is so ver - y near.

Copyright, 1896, by Hall-Mack Co.

MARCH WITH HAPPY SONG. Concluded.

while you sing for Christ the King, Hold-ing high the cross, the cross, He leads the way each pass-ing day, You'll nev-er suf-fer loss, no loss.

LOVING WORDS.

Adapted.   J. LINCOLN HALL.

1. Lov-ing words will cost but lit-tle, Journeying up the hill of life,
2. When the cares of life are ma-ny, And its burdens heav-y grow
3. So, as up life's hill we jour-ney, Let us scat-ter all the way

But they make the weak and wea-ry Stronger, brav-er for the strife.
For the ones who walk be-side you, If you love them, tell them so.
Kind-ly words, to serve as sun-shine In the dark and cloud-y day.

D.S. { Nev-er was a kind word wast-ed, Nev-er was one said in vain.
        And be-neath their cheering sun-shine Hearts will blossom like a flower.
        To the ones who jour-ney with you; If you love them, tell them so.

D.S.

Do you count them on-ly tri-fles? What on earth are sun and rain?
What you count of lit-tle val-ue Has an al-most mag-ic pow'r,
Grudge no lov-ing word, my broth-er, As a-long thro' life you go,

Copyright, 1896, by Hall-Mack Co.

THERE'S A FRIEND WE LOVE.

J. L. H. J. LINCOLN HALL.

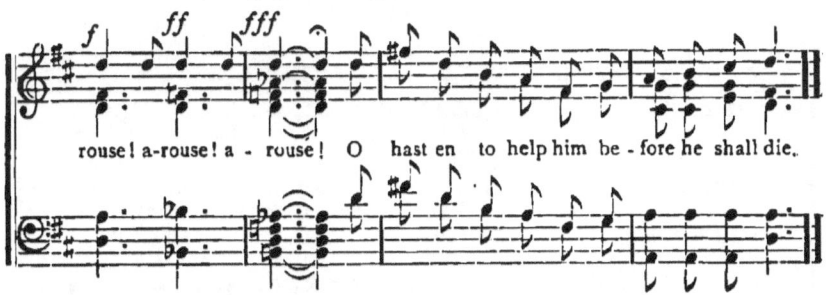

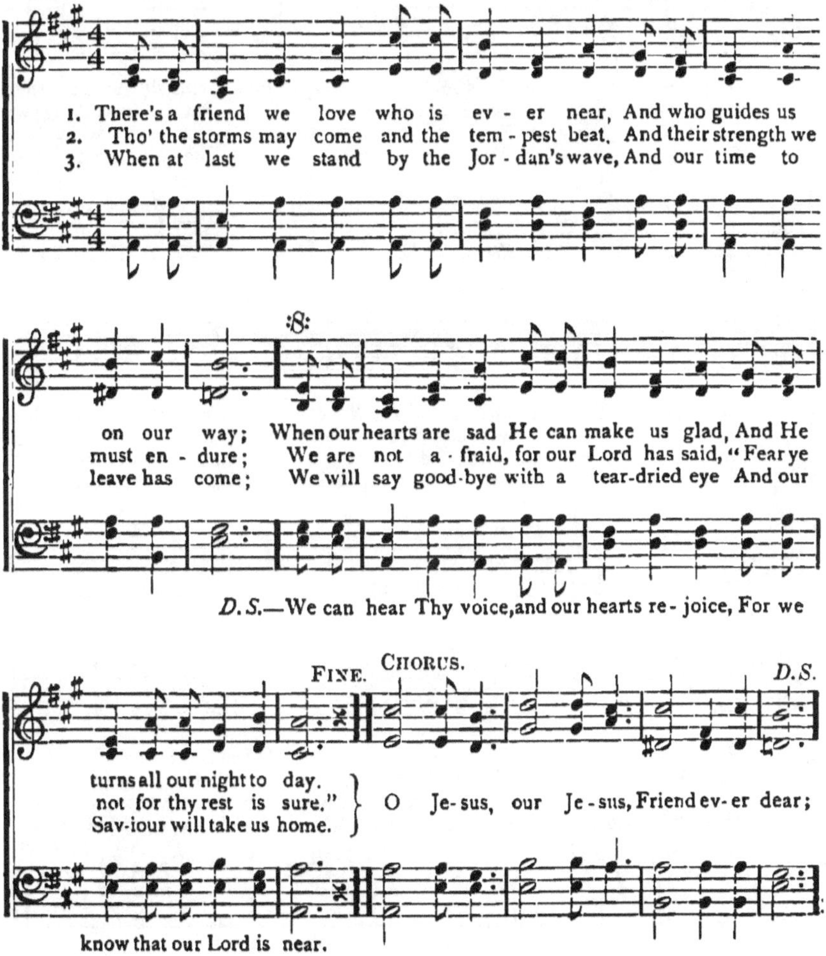

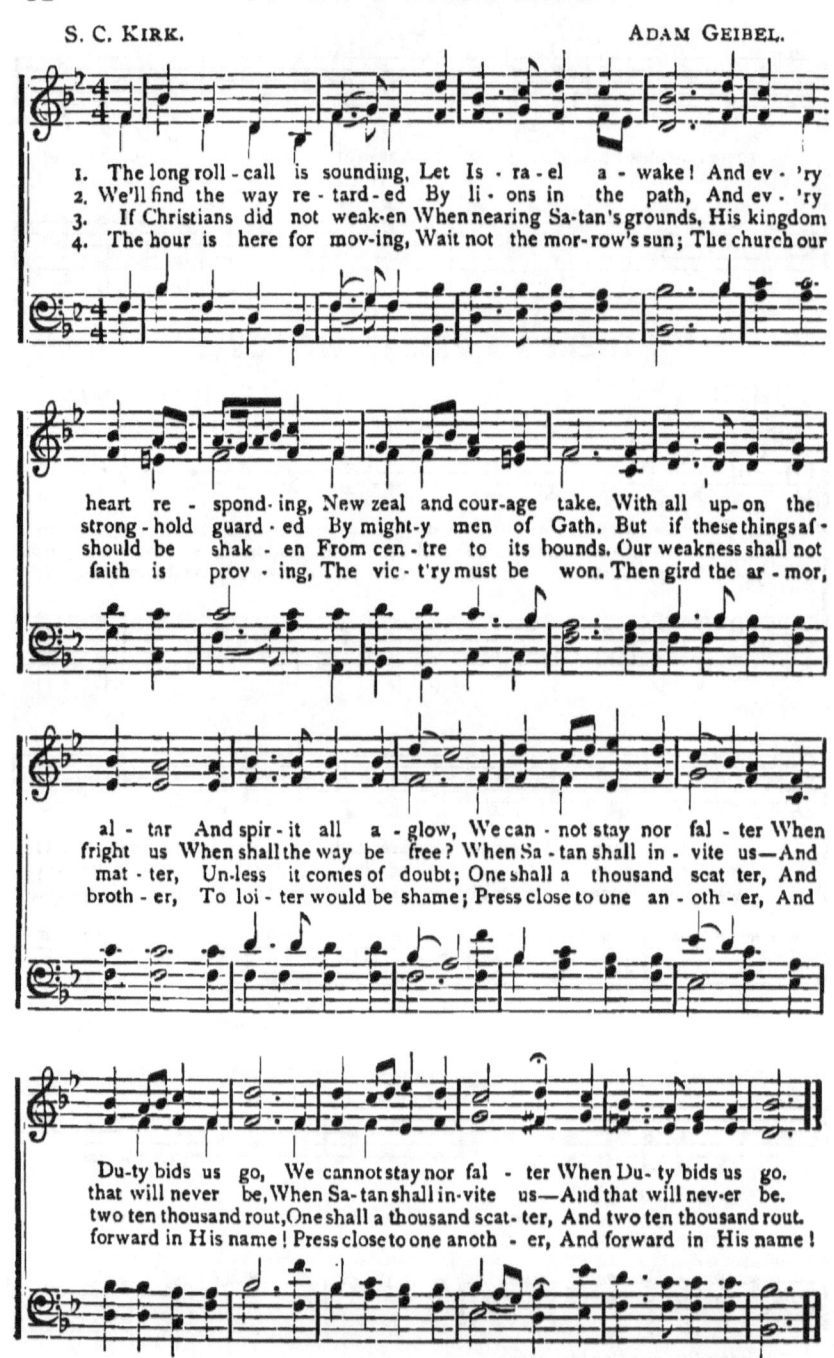

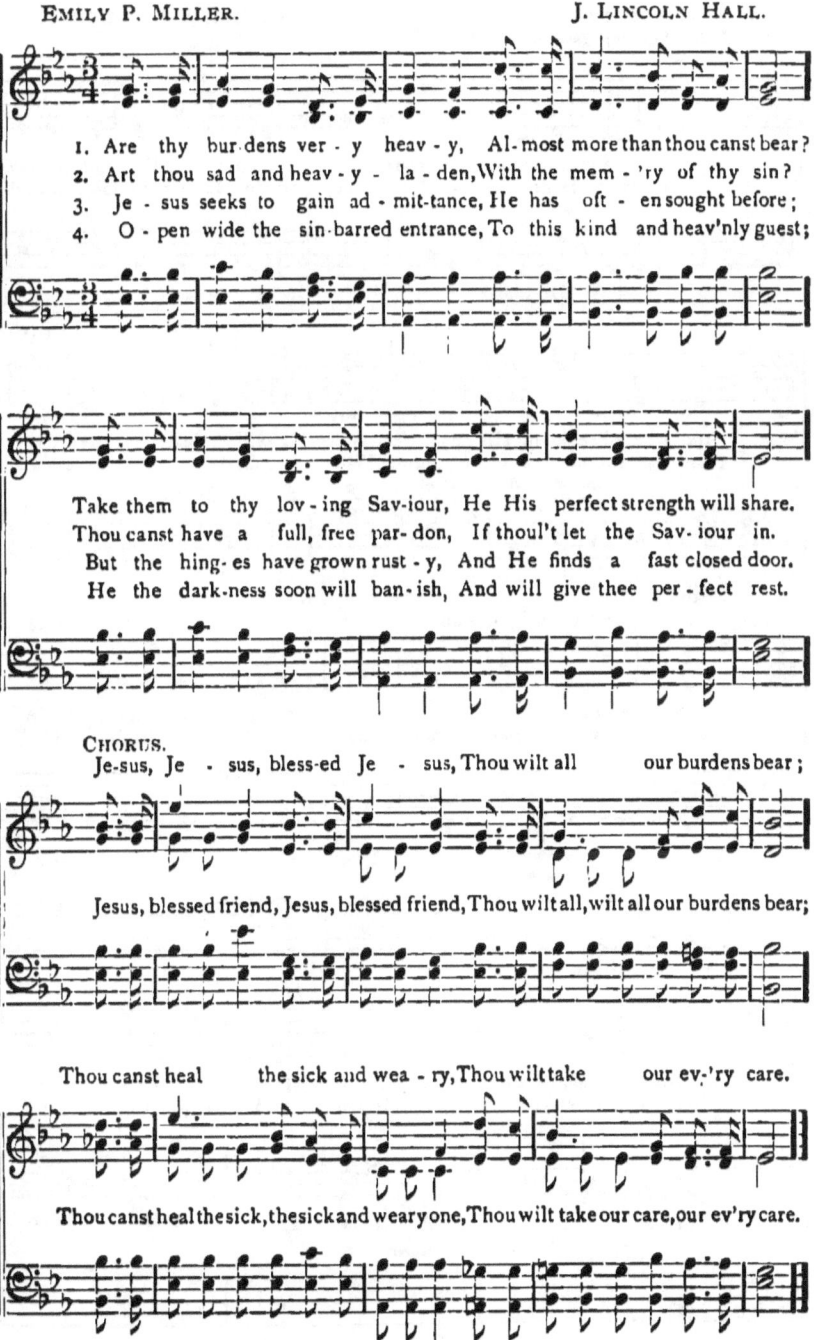

THE FRIEND OF FRIENDS. Concluded.

D. S. for last verse.

step a-right, To Him we cling, and trust Him still.
from the eye That watch-es o'er us ev-'ry-where.

THERE IS A BRIGHT AND HAPPY HOME.

Adapted. J. LINCOLN HALL.

1. There is a bright and hap-py home, Where all is joy and glad-ness,
2. This life is oft-en cloud-ed o'er, With tear-ful hours of sor-row,
3. There, all our fears are laid to rest, And hush'd is all our weep-ing,
4. We hope to reach this hap-py home, Where there is no more weep-ing,

Where sin and sor-row may not come, Nor an-y thought of sad-ness.
And those we hold so dear to-day, May go from us to-mor-row.
There, troubled hearts find sweet re-pose, Like lit-tle chil-dren sleep-ing.
But wait in pa-tience God's own time, We still are in his keep-ing.

*D.S.—*Where we shall dwell in God's own light, For ev-er and for ev-er.

D.S.

We love to think of that sweet home, Where death can part us nev-er,

Copyright, 1896, by Hall-Mack Co.

HAPPY SEASONS.

IRVIN H. MACK. FRANK L. ARMSTRONG.

1. In hap-py springtime forth we go, With hop-ing hearts the seeds to sow,
2. The hours and days go flit-ting by, The rays of sun are draw-ing nigh,
3. Be-hold how bright the fields ap pear, 'Neath summer sun which now is here,
4. The au-tumn leaves have come at last, The spring and sum-mer-time have past,

And ask the earth so kind and warm, To keep them safe from ev-'ry harm.
The smil-ing buds are peep-ing out, All na-ture lifts a thank-ful shout.
The fruit hangs heav-y ev-'ry where, That all may in its boun-ties share.
The glean-er's songs are sounding sweet, They sep-a-rate the tares from wheat.

REFRAIN.

Let chris-tian workers hear the call, 'Een now He's sounding forth to all,

Repeat ad lib.

The Sav iour bids us gar-ner in The sheaves of good from fields of sin.

Copyright, 1896, by Hall-Mack Co.

O JESUS, MY SAVIOUR. Concluded.

There at His feet your burdens lay—Each sorrow, grief and woe;
The fountain of His blood shall heal, The soul so sick and sore,
And cleanse from ev'ry taint of sin, To make it pure once more.

SWEET NAME OF JESUS.

G. KINGSLEY.

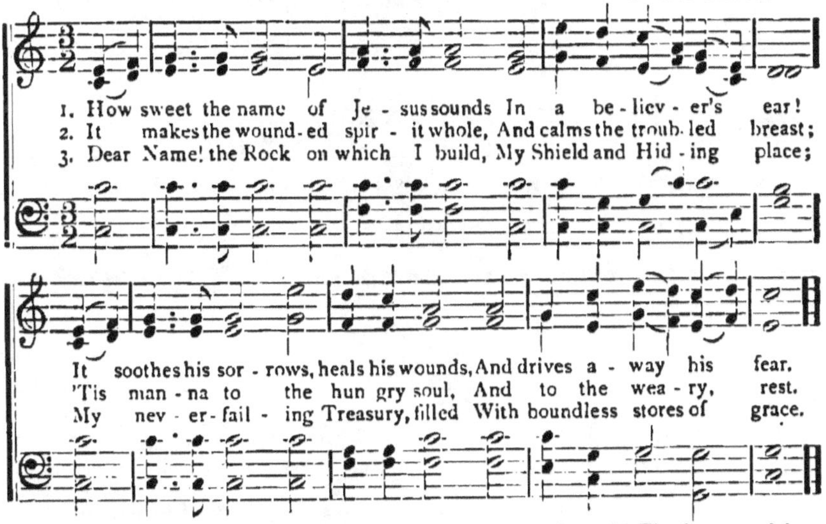

1. How sweet the name of Jesus sounds In a believer's ear!
2. It makes the wounded spirit whole, And calms the troubled breast;
3. Dear Name! the Rock on which I build, My Shield and Hiding place;

It soothes his sorrows, heals his wounds, And drives away his fear.
'Tis manna to the hungry soul, And to the weary, rest.
My never-failing Treasury, filled With boundless stores of grace.

4 Weak is the effort of my heart,
And cold my warmest thought;
But when I see Thee as Thou art,
I'll praise Thee as I ought.

5 Till then I would Thy love proclaim
With ev'ry fleeting breath;
And may the music of Thy name
Refresh my soul in death.

IN THE SHADOW OF THE ROCK. Concluded. 73

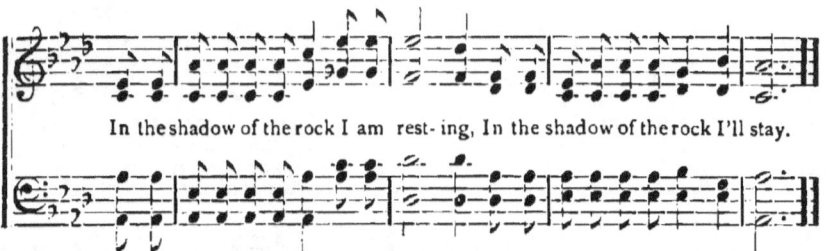

In the shadow of the rock I am rest-ing, In the shadow of the rock I'll stay.

FOR CHRIST'S SAKE.

M. S. HAYCRAFT. ARTHUR J. JAMOUNEAU.
Moderato.

1. Oh, for the sake of Christ the King Stretch forth a help-ing
2. Be thine the fall-ing tear to dry, The word of love to
3. Then at the time of glo-ry bright, The King shall speak to

hand; Thy suc-cor to the need-y bring, And cause the
say, To tell the sad a Friend is nigh, And com-fort
thee, "When to the heart in shades of night, Ye bore the

cres.   *rall.*

flow'rs of joy to spring A-cross the des-ert land.
breathe where spir-its sigh A-long life's pil-grim-way.
lamps of hope and light, Ye did it un-to me."

Copyright, 1896, by Hall-Mack Co.

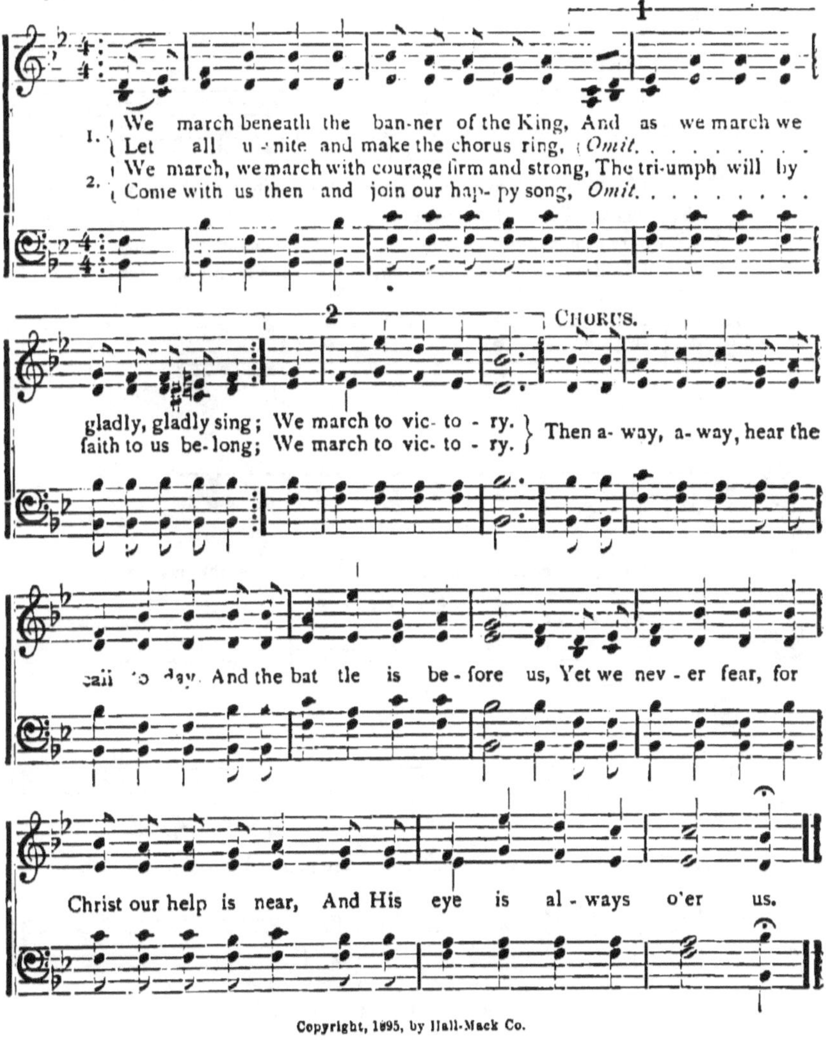

O PRODIGAL COME!   77

SILAS GRUBB. J. LINCOLN HALL.

1. O Prod-i-gal, Prod-i-gal, come home to-day, The Father now why long-er roam, A wel-come is wait-ing for thee—O come home.
2. O Prod-i-gal, Prod-i-gal, leave all thy sin, Come back to thy home, at the door en-ter in; O Prod-i-gal, Prod-i-gal, why stay a-way When mer-cy and par-don a-wait thee to-day.
3. O Prod-i-gal, Prod-i-gal, list to the call Which bids thee to cast a-way sin's bit-ter thrall, Come sit at the ta-ble now wait-ing for thee, Come back to thy Fa-ther, thy par-don is free.

REFRAIN.

O Prod-i-gal, Prod-i-gal, don't stay a-way, Come home, come home;
O Prod-i-gal, Prod-i-gal, come home to-day, Come home, come home, come home.

Copyright, 1896, by Hall-Mack Co.

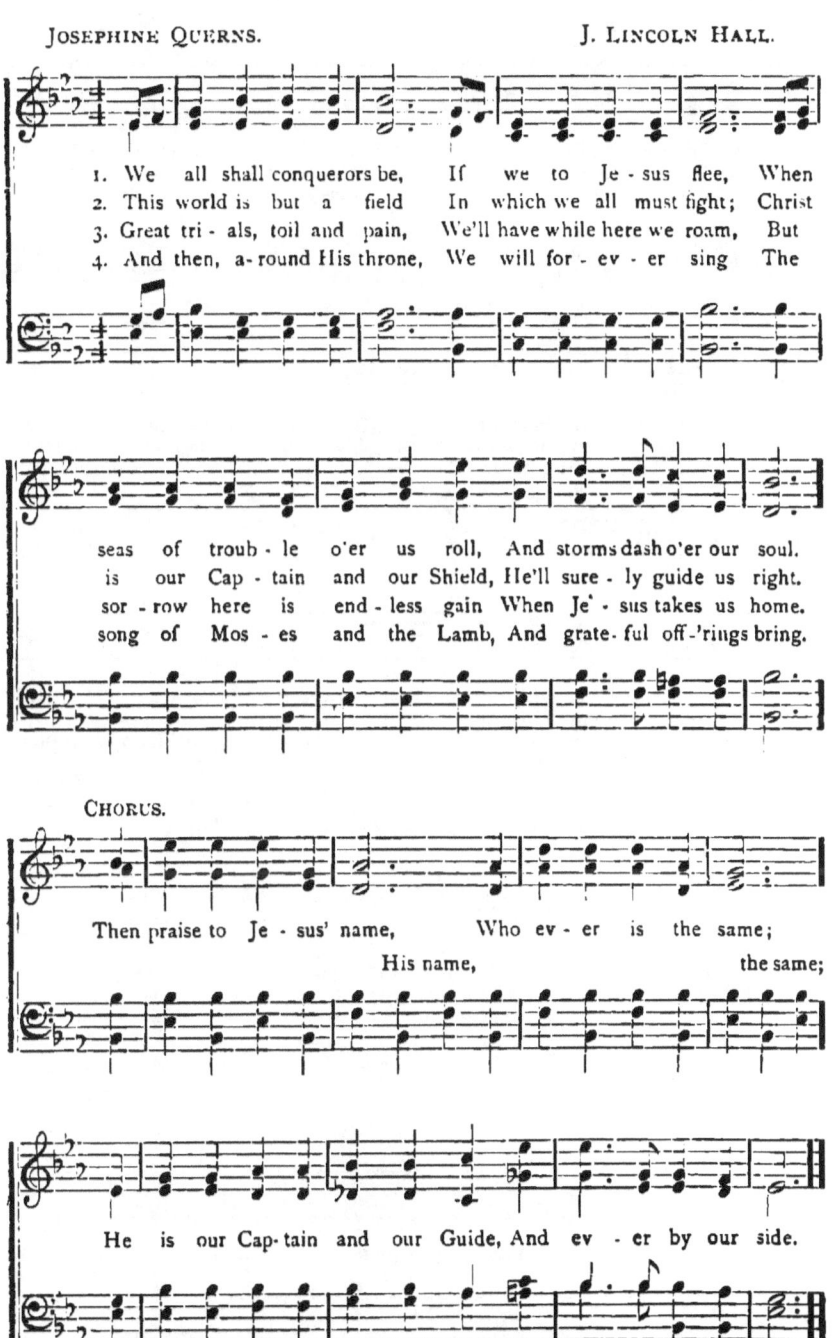

"DOST THOU CARE?"

JENNIE WILSON.   I. H. MEREDITH.

1. There are millions who have never Heard the sound of Jesus' name. Nor the
tid-ings that the Saviour To a-tone for sin-ners came. Faith's fair
light for us is shining While they dwell in sin's de-spair, Per-ish-
ing with-out the Gos-pel, Sis-ter, brother, dost thou care?

2. 'Tis the Saviour's last commandment, That His followers shall go In-to
all the world and wit-ness To the bless-ed truth they know. To the
Mas-ter's sol-emn bid-ding, Dost thou list-en or for-bear? From His
throne the Lord is watch-ing, Sis-ter, brother, dost thou care?

3. When the storms of time are over, In the land of ceaseless calm, Soon the
faith-ful ones will gath-er To the sup-per of the Lamb. Each true
ser-vant of the Mas-ter In that marriage feast shall share, Will there
be for thee a por-tion? Sis-ter, brother, dost thou care?

CHORUS.

Sis-ter, brother, dost thou care? Sis-ter, brother, dost thou care?

Copyright, 1895, I. H. Meredith.

DOST THOU CARE? Concluded.

Per-ish-ing with-out the gos-pel, Sis-ter, brother, dost thou care?

COME INTO THE ARK.

CARRIE ELLIS BRECK.
I. HICKMAN MEREDITH.

1. When blighting and sor-row shall fall on your soul, When skies shall be stormy and dark,
2. The Saviour has call'd you again and a-gain, Oh sin-ner stay not in your flight,
3. Come sin-ner no long-er your fol-lies pur-sue, Oh will you not haste to em-bark.

When wild flooding wa-ters shall o-ver you roll, Oh will you be safe in the ark?
For sud-den de-struc-tion shall come up-on men, As com-eth a thief in the night.
While Je-sus is ten-der-ly call-ing to you, Come in—O come in-to the ark.

CHORUS.

Come in-to the ark come in, come in, Come in-to the ark and be saved;

Come in-to the ark of God's mercy to-day, Come in-to the ark and be saved.

Copyright, 1895, by I. Hickman Meredith.

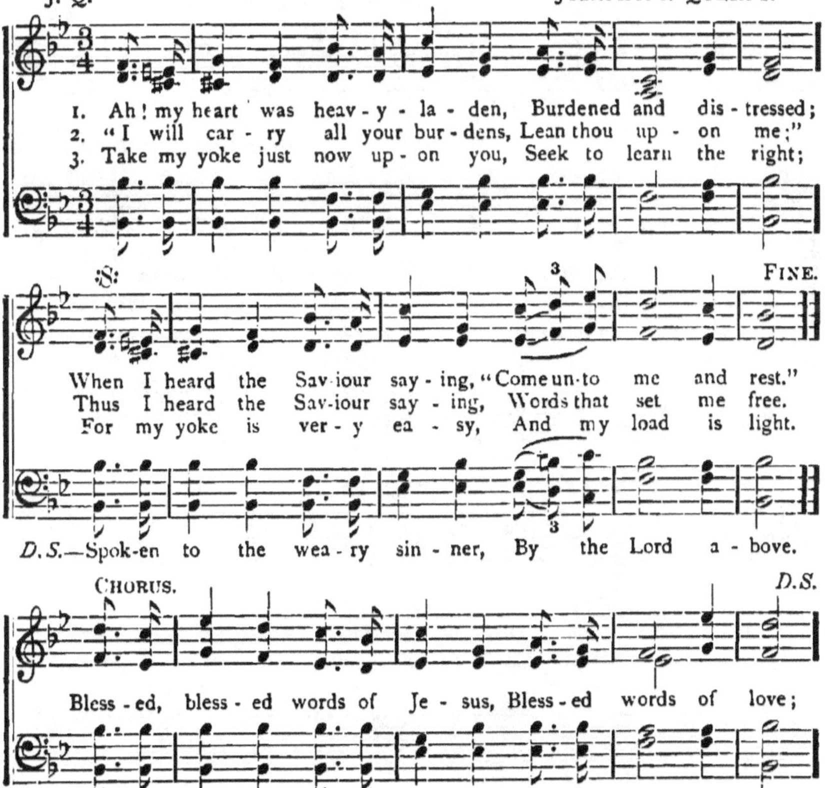

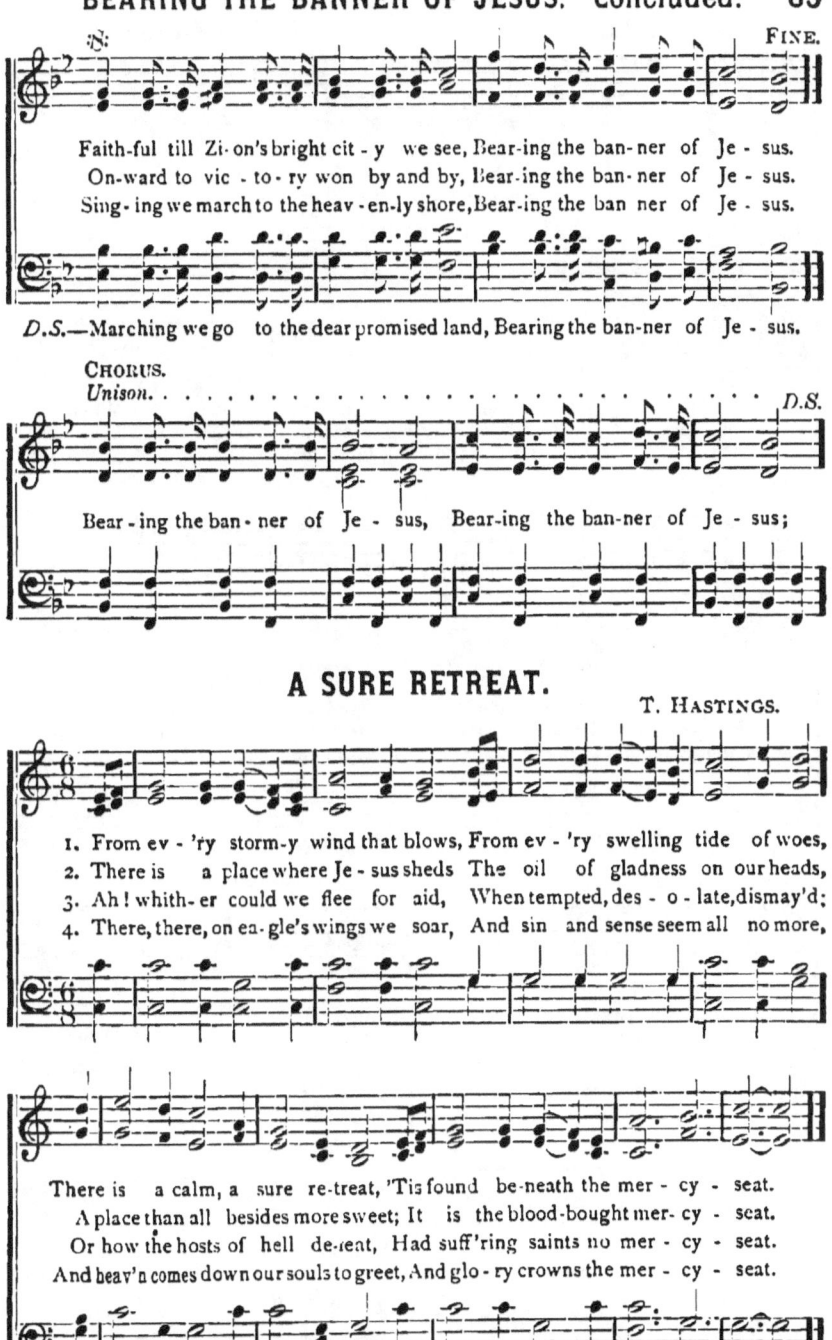

IN THAT DAY. Concluded.

CHRISTIAN CHILDREN MUST BE HOLY.

ITHAMAR CONKEY.

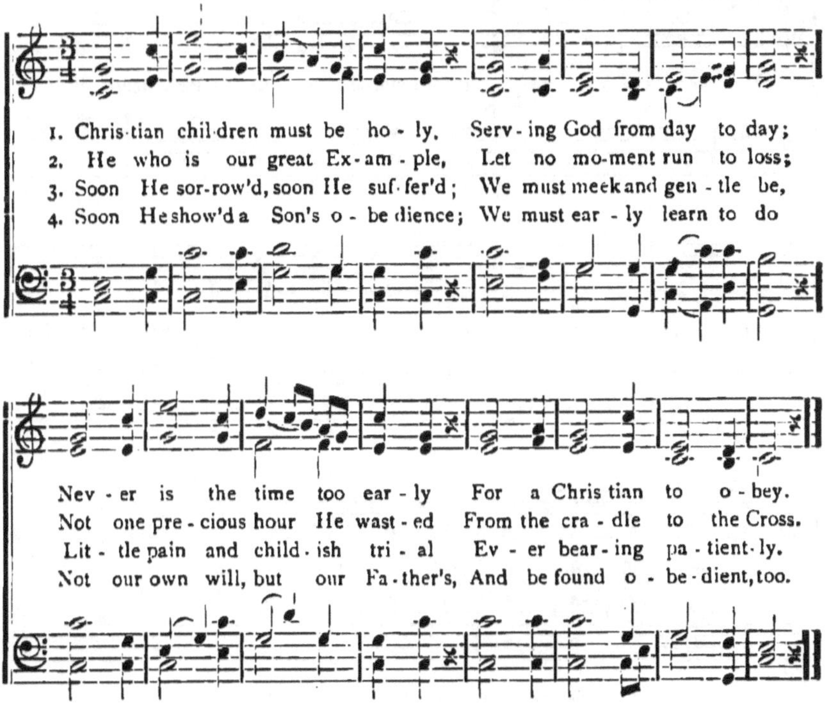

1. Chris-tian chil-dren must be ho - ly, Serv - ing God from day to day;
2. He who is our great Ex - am - ple, Let no mo-ment run to loss;
3. Soon He sor-row'd, soon He suf-fer'd; We must meek and gen - tle be,
4. Soon He show'd a Son's o - be dience; We must ear - ly learn to do

Nev - er is the time too ear - ly For a Chris tian to o - bey.
Not one pre - cious hour He wast - ed From the cra - dle to the Cross.
Lit - tle pain and child - ish tri - al Ev - er bear - ing pa - tient-ly.
Not our own will, but our Fa-ther's, And be found o - be - dient, too.

WE PASS THIS WAY BUT ONCE.   89

AMANDA R. MEUSCH.   FRANK M. DAVIS, by per.

1. As we jour-ney on our pathway, Which thro' life's great valley leads;
2. Let us help the wea ry pilgrim, Whom we meet up-on our way,
3. Let us not de-lay our actions, Thoughtless for an oth-er day;

Let us scat-ter seeds of kindness, Strew our path with lov-ing deeds.
With a kind-ly word and ac tion, With a lov-ing deed to-day.
There are souls that must be rescued, Let us help them while we may.

CHORUS.

We pass . . . . . this way but once, We
We pass this way,   this way but once,

pass . . . . . this way but once;   Let us
We pass this way,   this way but once; Let us

scat ter   seeds of kindness,   For we pass this way but once.
scatter seeds of kindness, scatter seeds of kindness,

Copyright, 1896, by Frank M. Davis.

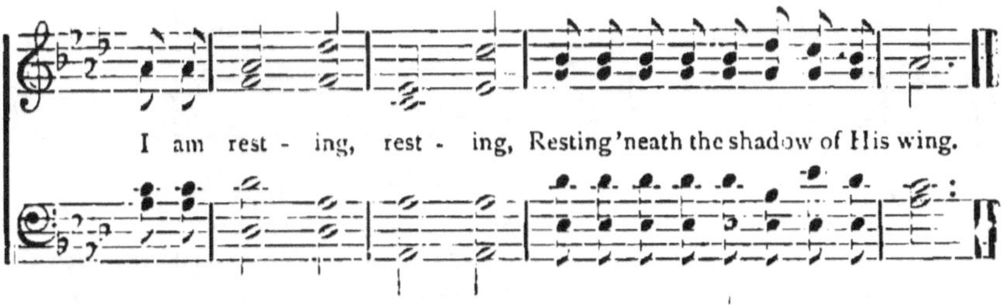

THE SHADOW OF HIS WING. Concluded.

I am rest - ing, rest - ing, Resting 'neath the shadow of His wing.

TRUSTING GOD.

W. Smith.
Charles Bentley.

1. Now that my jour ney's just be-gun; My course so lit - tle trod—
2. If all my earthly friends should die, And leave me mourning here—
3. And Lord, what ev - er grief or ill For me may be in store,

I'll stay be - fore I fur - ther go, And give my self to God:
Since God re-gards the or phan's cry— Oh! what have I to fear?
Make me sub-mis - sive to Thy will, And I would ask no more:

But if the Lord will be my friend, I know that all is well.
He feeds the rav - ens when they cry, And fills His poor with bread.
And when I'm fee - ble, old and gray, Oh! God, for-sake me not.

What sor - rows may my steps at tend, I can - not now for - tell:
If I am poor He can sup - ply—Who hath my ta - ble spread;
And all the way be Thou my stay, What-ev - er be my lot,

Copyright, 1896, by Charles Bentley.

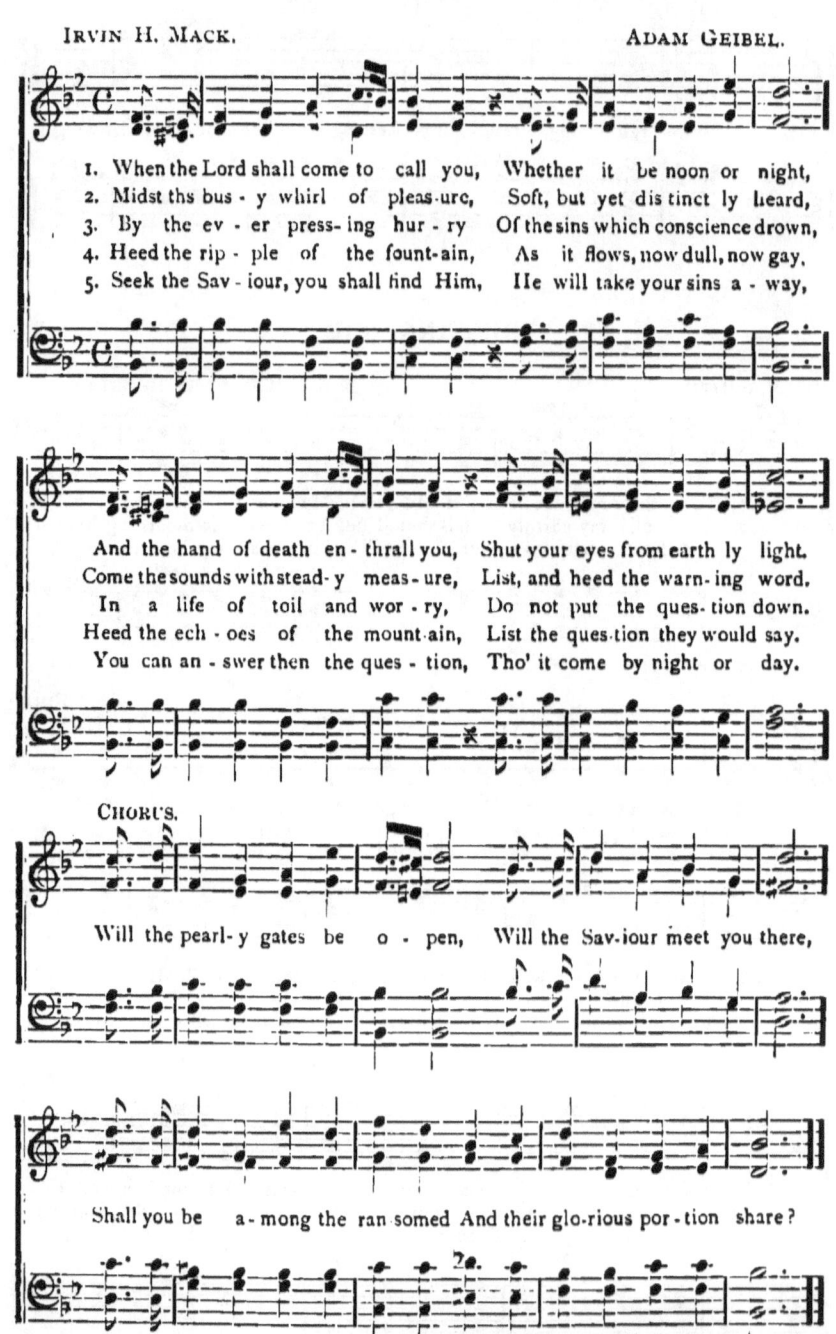

94 THE CHRISTIAN PATH.

Words arr. by IRVIN H. MACK.   J. LINCOLN HALL.

1. Do not de-spise the chris-tian path That ma-ny faith-ful tread;
2. Go strive with-in the world of gloom, To shed what light you may;
3. Do not a-void the chris tian path, Go do some deed of good;
4. How ma-ny souls that walked this path, Their hearts to Je-sus giv'n,
5. Do not for-sake the chris-tian path, Its joys will all be thine,

But join the ranks with will-ing hearts, For Christ is at the head.
Re-mem-ber that a flow'r may bloom, 'Neath sunshine's smallest ray.
Tho' small it be, re-mem-ber, 'tis By Je-sus un-der-stood.
Have swept a-cross the Jor-dan's tide With-in the gates of heav'n.
And you shall dwell with Christ in heav'n; Forev-er there to shine.

CHORUS.

O let us walk in the paths of righteousness, O go with stead-y tread,

Let no one fal-ter by the way, For Christ is at the head.

Copyright, 1896 by Hall-Mack Co.

LIVING FOR JESUS.

HARRY MACK.   J. LINCOLN HALL.

SOLO or *Voices in Unison.* (*Slowly.*)

1. A little brook that murmurs lowly, A little stream that trickles slowly Shall some day reach old ocean's brine, Shall reach old ocean's brine: A little Samuel, living solely To minister in office holy, Becomes a messenger divine, A messenger divine.
2. A little light' tho' dimly flashing A-cross the waters, wild and dashing, Will guide the sails thro' storm and tide, Will guide thro' storm and tide: A little life on God reclining, Up-on the sea of turmoil shining, Will tell salvation far and wide, Salvation far and wide.
3. A little isolated flower, In beauty, breathes its fragrant power; And charms the trav-'ler on the way, And charms him on the way; The little stars, unseen at twilight Be-deck the lofty vaults with skylight Un-til the dawning of the day, The dawning of the day.

CHORUS. *Unison. Faster.*

A little act is but the seed Of great and glorious

Copyrighted, 1896, by Hall-Mack Co.

LIVING FOR JESUS.—Concluded.

ends; A lit-tle fact sup-plies the needs of him, who heav'ward wends.

HAPPY CHILDREN ARE WE.

EMILY P. MILLER. HOWARD CLARE.

1. We are hap-py child-ren On this joy-ous day, Birds are sweetly
2. Let us then a-dore Him, Christ the Lord of all, Glad-ly bring our
3. We are hap-py child-ren Of the Heav'nly King, Glad-ly let us
4. Tell-ing of His mer-cy, And His wondrous love, And the precious

CHORUS.

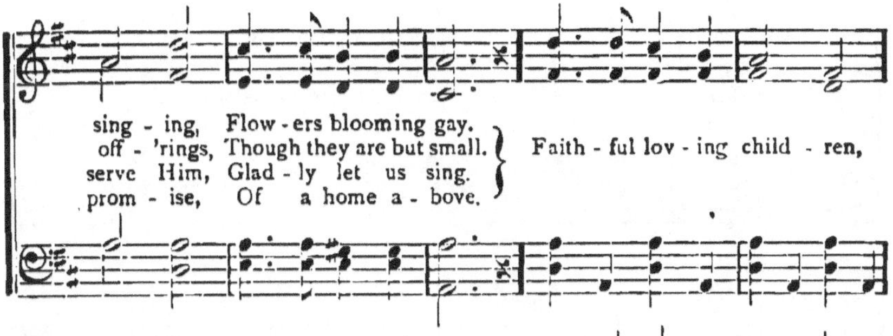

sing-ing, Flow-ers blooming gay.
off-'rings, Though they are but small.
serve Him, Glad-ly let us sing.
prom-ise, Of a home a-bove.

Faith-ful lov-ing child-ren, Ev-er we must be, If we wish to serve Him Thro' e-ter-ni-ty.

Copyrighted, 1896, by Hall-Mack Co.

98. THE EARLY PRIMROSE.

Adapted.   FRANK L. ARMSTRONG.

1. I love the ear-ly prim-rose That light-ens up the lane,
   So ra-diant in the sun-shine, So cheer-ful aft-er rain.
   "Good-bye to drea-ry win-ter," How glad-ly doth it sing,
   And tells of mild-er weath-er, And hope-ful, hap-py spring.

2. I wish that like the prim-rose My life were al-ways bright,
   And shone in dark-est path-ways With mild and con-stant light;
   I wish that I re-flect-ed Each sun-ray from a-bove,
   I wish that 'neath the storm cloud I al-ways smiled with love.

3. I wish that in the val-ley As on the swell-ing hill,
   Seen, or un-seen, with beau-ty I did my task ful-fill;
   In life's se-clu-ded cop-ses As in the gar-den gay,
   Be-side the for-est foot-track As by the broad high-way.

4. I would be ev-er show-ing That win-ter's reign is o'er;
   A hap-py pledge and prom-ise Of joys for-ev-er-more;
   I would be like the prim-rose, And sing, in sun or shade,
   Of spring the ev-er-last-ing, Of flow'rs that nev-er fade.

Copyright, 1896, by Frank L. Armstrong.

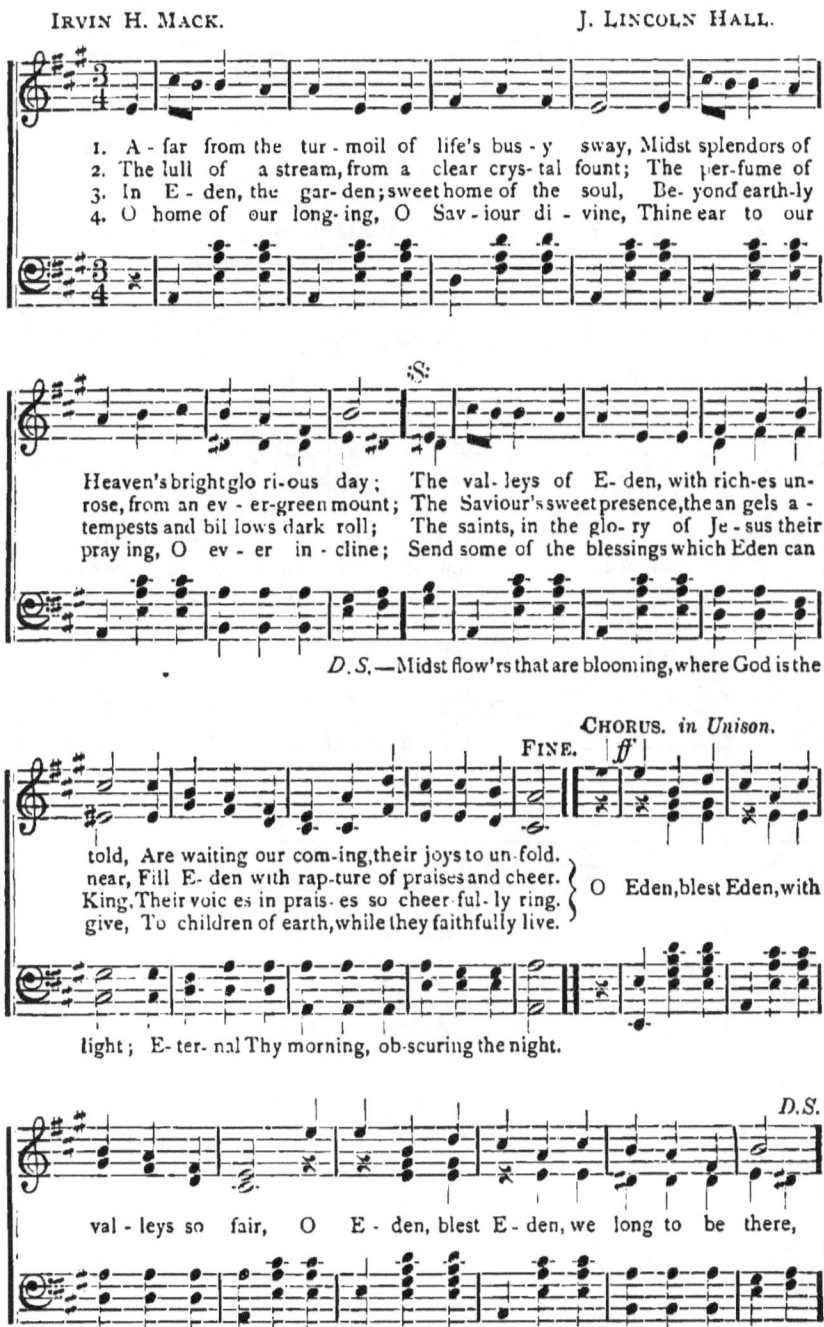

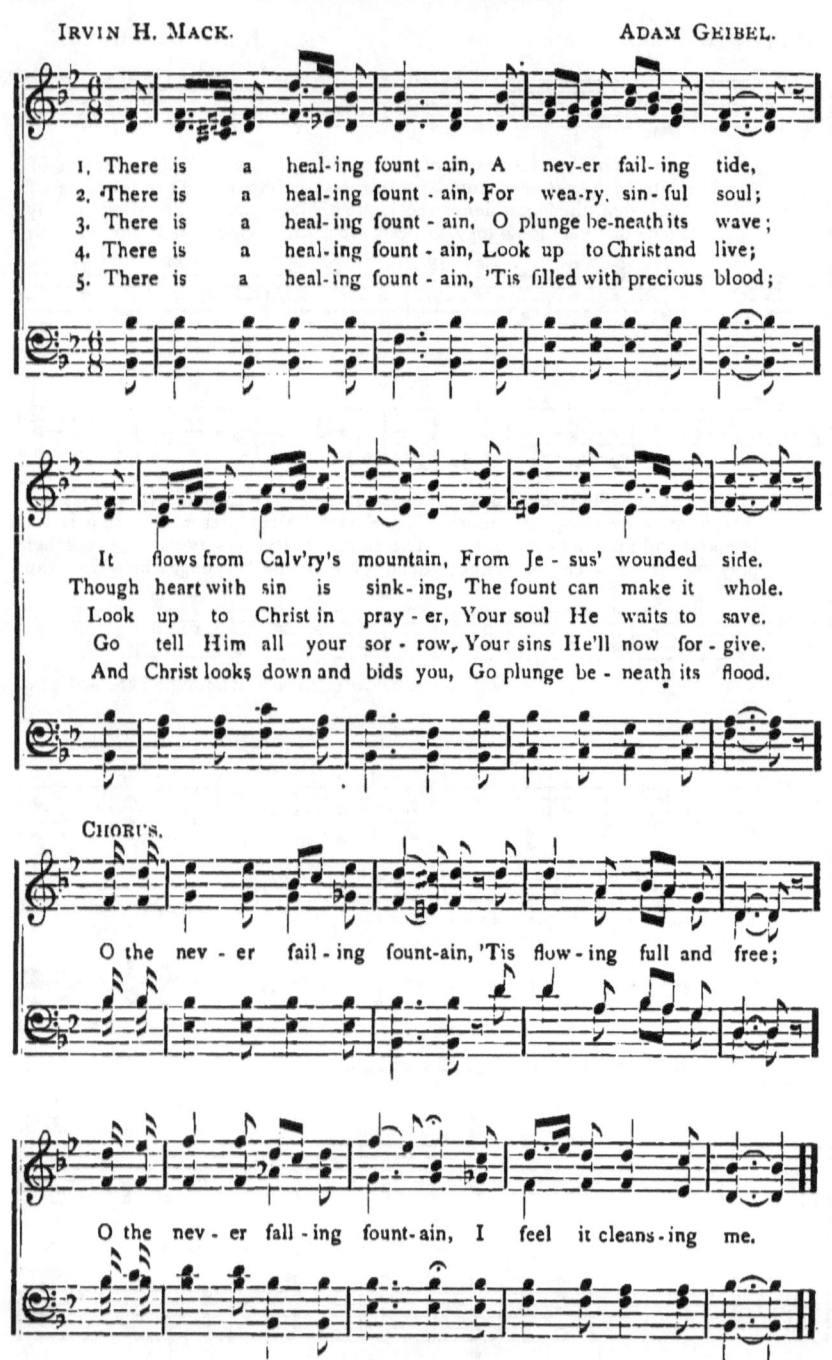

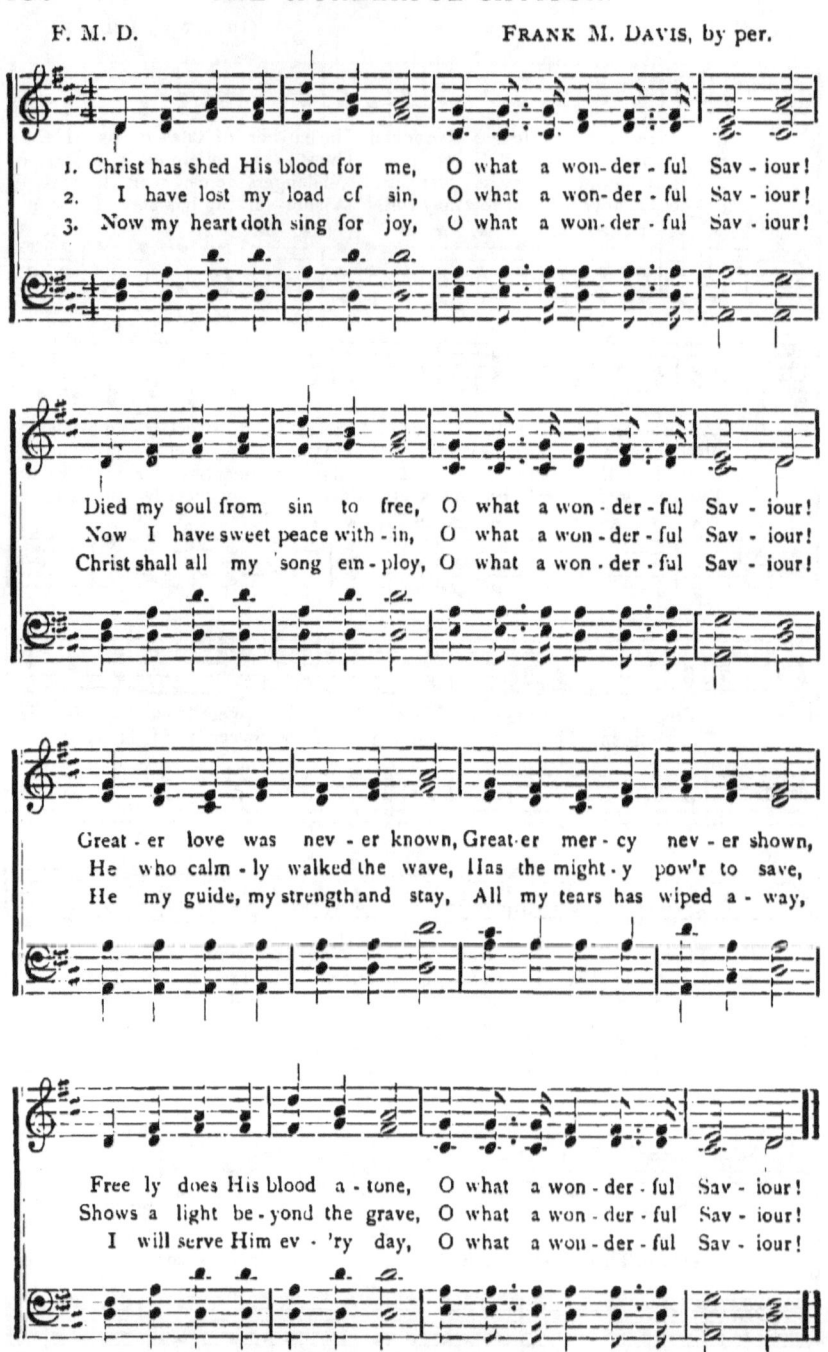

AND SHALL I TURN BACK? 105

Arr. by GRACE WEISER DAVIS.

1. My Jesus, I love Thee, I know Thou art mine, For Thee all the follies of sin I resign; My gracious Redeemer, my Saviour art Thou; If ever I loved Thee, my Jesus, 'tis now.
2. I love Thee because Thou hast first loved me, And purchased my pardon on Calvary's tree; I love Thee for wearing the thorns on Thy brow; If ever I loved Thee, my Jesus, 'tis now.
3. I'll love Thee in life, I will love Thee in death, And praise Thee as long as Thou givest me breath, And say when the death-dew lies cold on my brow; If ever I loved Thee, my Jesus, 'tis now.
4. In mansions of glory and endless delight, I'll ever adore Thee in heaven so bright; I'll sing with the glittering crown on my brow; If ever I loved Thee, my Jesus, 'tis now.

CHORUS.

And shall I turn back into the world? O, no, not I, not I!
I'll never turn back, never turn back, O, no, not I, not I!
And shall I turn back into the world? No, no, not I!
I'll never turn back, never turn back, O, no, not I! . . .

Copyright, 1894, by Grace Weiser Davis. Used by per.

THE FLIGHT OF TIME.

HARRY MACK. J. LINCOLN HALL.

1. Tick by tick, the mo-ments fleeting Measure out the pass-ing day;
2. Month by month, in wax-ing, waning; Comes and goes the sil-ver moon:

While the rap-id pulse is beat-ing, Slips our pre-cious life a-way.
So we know the strength we're gaining Turns and weak-ens all too soon.

GIRLS.

Hour by hour, the bell is toll - ing, Some one 'sorrow, some fare - well;
Year by year, our lives are ag - ing, Treading on-ward to the grave;

BOYS.   ALL PARTS. *Use 1st four lines as Cho.* D.C.

List, its tones so deeply roll - ing Sound a-broad a part ing knell.
Fleeting hopes the heart engag - ing, Time o'ertakes the bold and brave.

Copyrighted, 1896, by Hall-Mack Co.

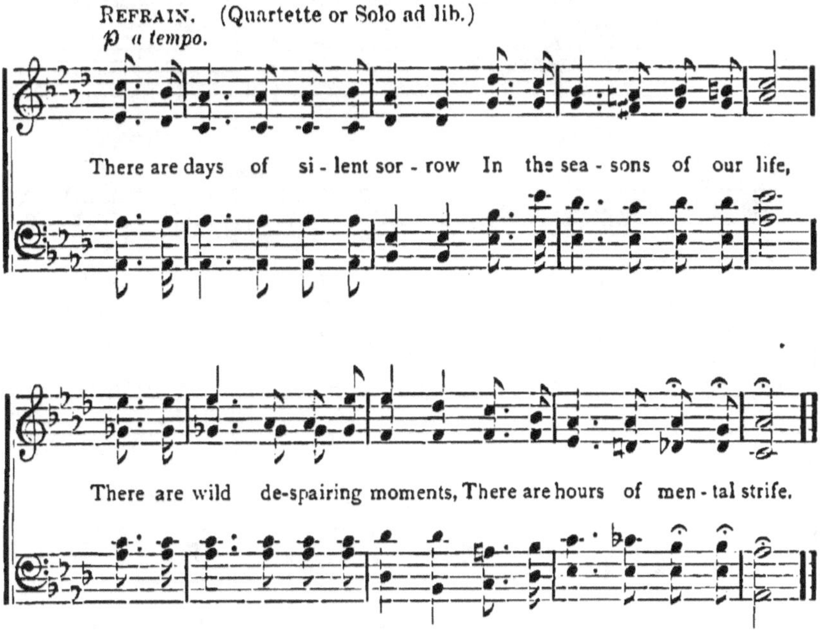

THE WAITING TIME. Concluded. 109

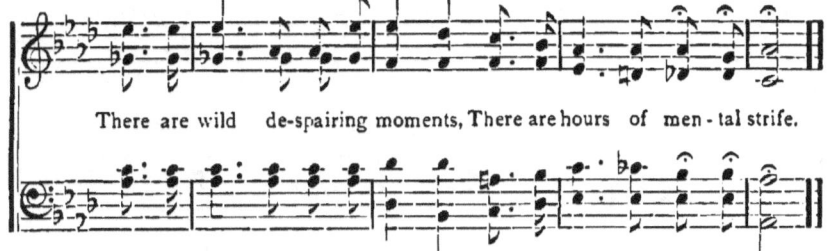

fall; But the waiting time, my brothers, Is the hardest time of all.
fall; And the waiting time, my brothers, Is the hardest time of all.
fall; But the waiting time, my brothers, Is the hardest time of all.

REFRAIN. (Quartette or Solo ad lib.)
p a tempo.

There are days of silent sorrow In the seasons of our life,

There are wild despairing moments, There are hours of mental strife.

4 For it wears the eager spirit
   As the salt waves wear the stone,
And the garb of hope grows threadbare
   Till the brighter tints are flown;
Then amid youth's radiant tresses
   Silent snows begin to fall;
Oh, the waiting time, my brothers,
   Is the hardest time of all!

5 But at last we learn the lesson
   That God knoweth what is best;
For with wisdom cometh patience,
   And with patience cometh rest.
Yea, a golden thread is shining
   Through the tangled woof of fate;
And our hearts shall thank him meekly,
   That he taught us how to wait.

110 THE SONG OF LOVE.

HARRIET E. JONES.   I. H. MEREDITH.

1. There are songs, sweet songs, that I love to hear, When my heart is sad and the way is drear, But the sweet-est song, that has come to me, Is the glad new song of the soul set free; O that song so sweet, O that song so sweet, From the new-born soul at the mer-cy seat, Like the
2. In the bright glad years of the long a-go, From the moth-er lips in a gen-tle flow, Came a song of peace, with a sweet re-frain, Like the round full notes of the spring birds strain, But the song so sweet, which the saved re-peat, When the Lord is found at the mer-cy seat, Brings more
3. When we reach our home, on the E-den-side, Where the blood wash'd throng, with the King, a-bide, Then the song first learn'd at the mer-cy seat, To the King of kings we will each re-peat, O that song so sweet, O that song so sweet, That we learn'd to sing at the mer-cy seat, We will

REFRAIN.

Copyright, 1894, by I. H. Meredith. Used by per.

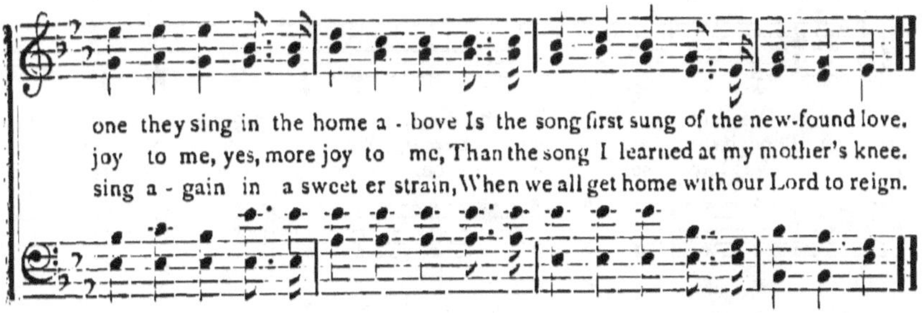

THE SONG OF LOVE. Concluded. 111

one they sing in the home a-bove Is the song first sung of the new-found love.
joy to me, yes, more joy to me, Than the song I learned at my mother's knee.
sing a-gain in a sweet-er strain, When we all get home with our Lord to reign.

COME, THOU ALMIGHTY KING!

CHARLES WESLEY. FELICE GIARDINI.

1. Come, Thou Al-might-y King, Help us Thy name to sing,
2. Come, Thou in-car-nate Word, Gird on Thy might-y sword;
3. Come, ho-ly Com-fort-er! Thy sa-cred wit-ness bear,

Help us to praise; Fa-ther! all-glo-ri-ous, O'er all vic-
Our pray'r at-tend; Come, and Thy peo-ple bless, And give Thy
In this glad hour; Thou, who al-might-y art, Now rule in

to-ri-ous, Come, and reign o-ver us, An-cient of Day!
word suc-cess, Spir-it of ho-li-ness! On us de-scend.
ev-'ry heart, And ne'er from us de-part, Spir-it of pow'r!

BATTLING FOR THE LORD. Concluded. 113

D.S.

shout our bat-tle cry, Let us keep our ar-mour bright, As we

THE BEAUTIFUL SUNSHINE.

F. M. D.   Frank M. Davis, by per.

1. Je - sus, the beau - ti - ful sun - shine, Changing the night in - to day,
2. Je - sus, the beau - ti - ful sun - shine, Shining from portals a - bove,
3. Je - sus, the beau - ti - ful sun - shine, Shine in our lives ev - er - more,

Shed in our hearts Thy bright radiance, Sweet-ly il - lu-mine our way.
When all around us is dark-ness, Send us a gleam of Thy love.
May we re-flect Thy ef - ful - gence, As we have nev-er be - fore.

CHORUS.

Sun - shine, sun - shine, Je - sus, the beau - ti - ful sun - shine;

Sun - shine, sun - shine, Sweet-ly il - lu-mine our way.

Copyright, 1896, by Frank M. Davis.

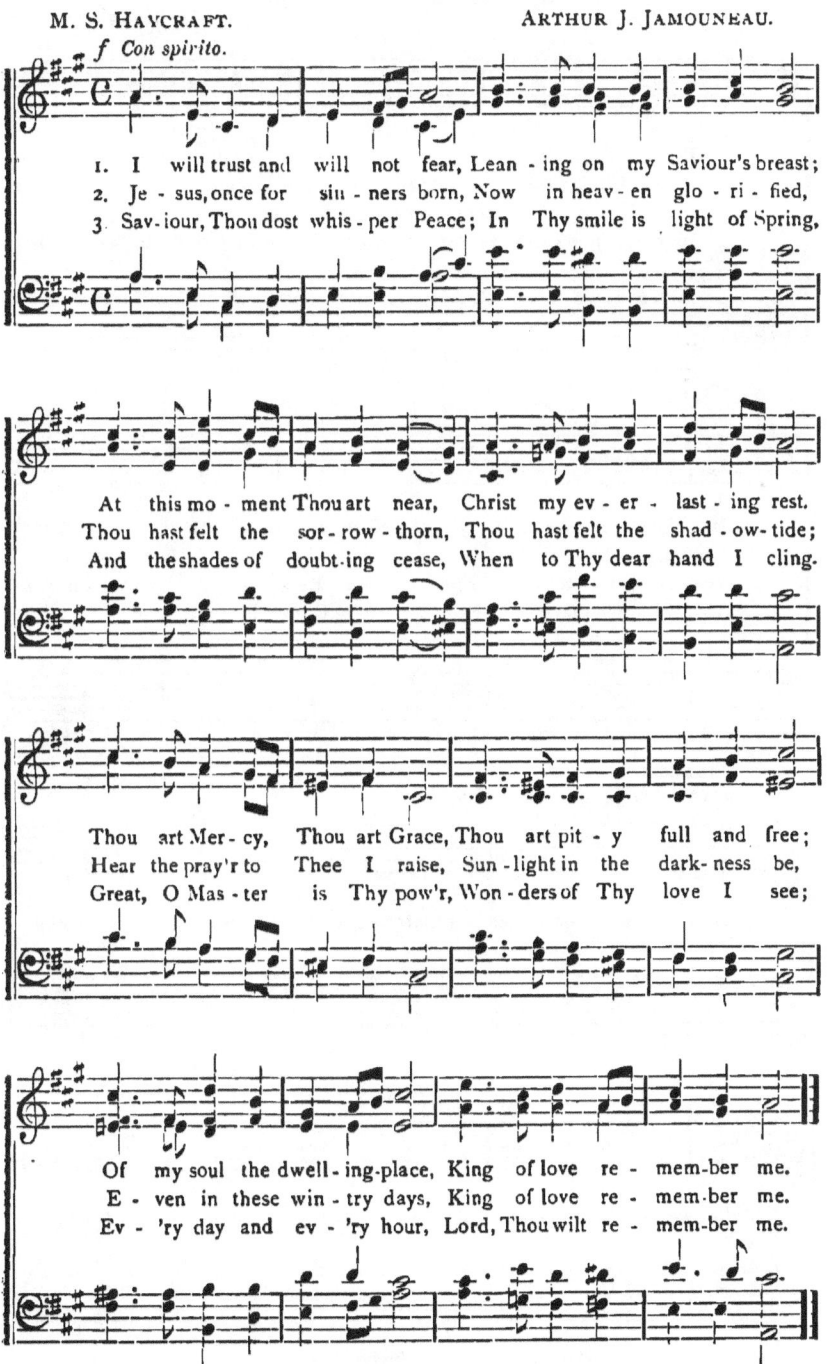

OBEY HIS COMMAND AND DO RIGHT.   117

C. B.   CHARLES BENTLEY.

1. My friends let me say that where-ev-er you go, God's spir-it will give you true light; Es-cape the temp-ta-tions, that lead thee a-stray,
2. God's teach-ing is plain, why should you re-fuse, The prom-ise that gives us de-light; Sal-va-tion gives free-dom to all who be-lieve,
3. The joy of sal-va-tion is heav-en to gain, Its pleas-ures are charming and bright; The bless-ed Re-deem-er has prom-ised to keep—
4. Ye wea-ry ones wres-tle as Ja-cob once did, Be read-y to wel-come the light; Oh think of the fav-ours He of-fers to you—

CHORUS.

O-bey His command and do right. Oh sin-ner you think it is hard to be good, Your conscience will tell you a-right, That christians are hap-py while liv-ing be-low,—O-bey His com-mand and do right.

Copyright, 1896, by Charles Bentley.

WILL YOU BE ONE? Concluded.

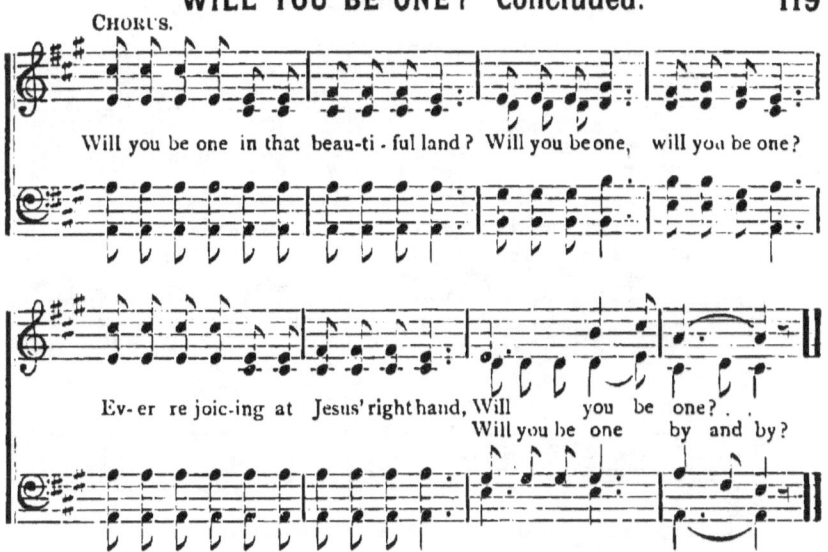

THE TEMPERANCE BANNER.

F. L. ARMSTRONG.

2 Come, join the noble army,
  Enlist now for the fight;
Maintain our nation's honor,
  Firm stand ye for the right.
Promote the cause of Temperance,
  To aid poor fallen man;
Put on the glorious armor,
  Be foremast in the van.

3 Then rally round the standard,
  And let the work go on
Until the last dim vestige
  Of intemperance is gone.
Be earnest in the battle,
  Your weapons boldly wield;
You'll surely gain the victory,
  And make the monster yield.

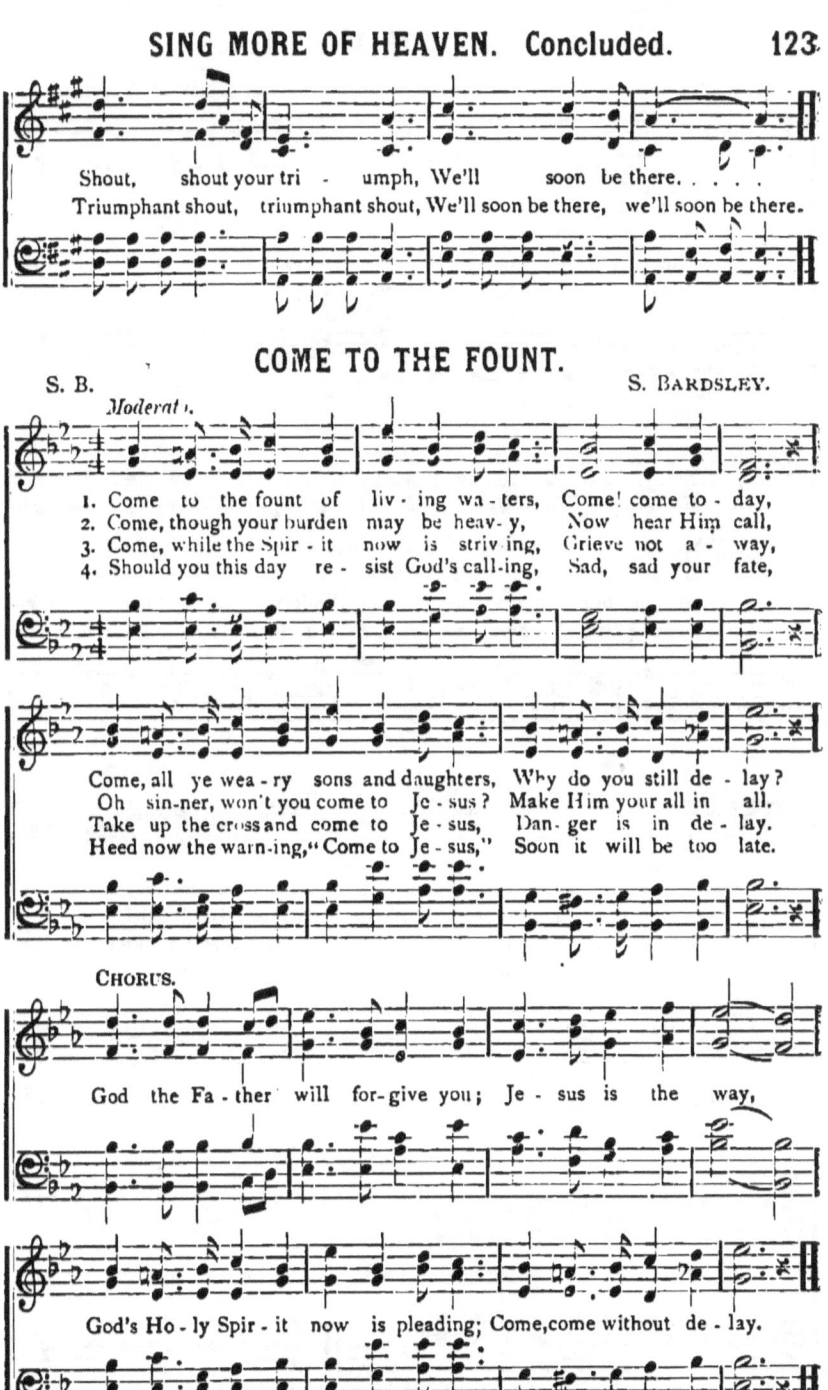

BE READY FOR THE CALL. Concluded. 125

Morning, noon or night; Have on the wedding garments and your lamps burning bright.

A SONG OF JOY, HOPE AND TRUST.

IRVIN H. MACK. ADAM GEIBEL.

1. I have a song with-in my heart, A song of joy di-vine,
2. I have a song with-in my heart, A song I love to sing,
3. I have a song with-in my heart, I'll sing from morn till night,

It came when first I learned to know, That Je-sus Christ was mine.
It is a song of glo-rious trust, A hope on which I cling,
A hap-py, bless-ed song of trust, From Je-sus I re-ceive.

How bright this dis-mal world ap-peared, I oft re-call the time,
The Sav-iour spake the words of love, Just now I hear them ring,
He fills me with a pow'r di-vine, He bids me e'er be-lieve,

E'en now my heart is filled with joy, For Je-sus Christ is mine.
Which made me free from ev-'ry sin, And Je-sus for my King.
All sin-ners with a weight of woe, He, on-ly, can re-lieve.

Copyright, 1896, by Hall-Mack Co.

FOR EVERMORE. Concluded.

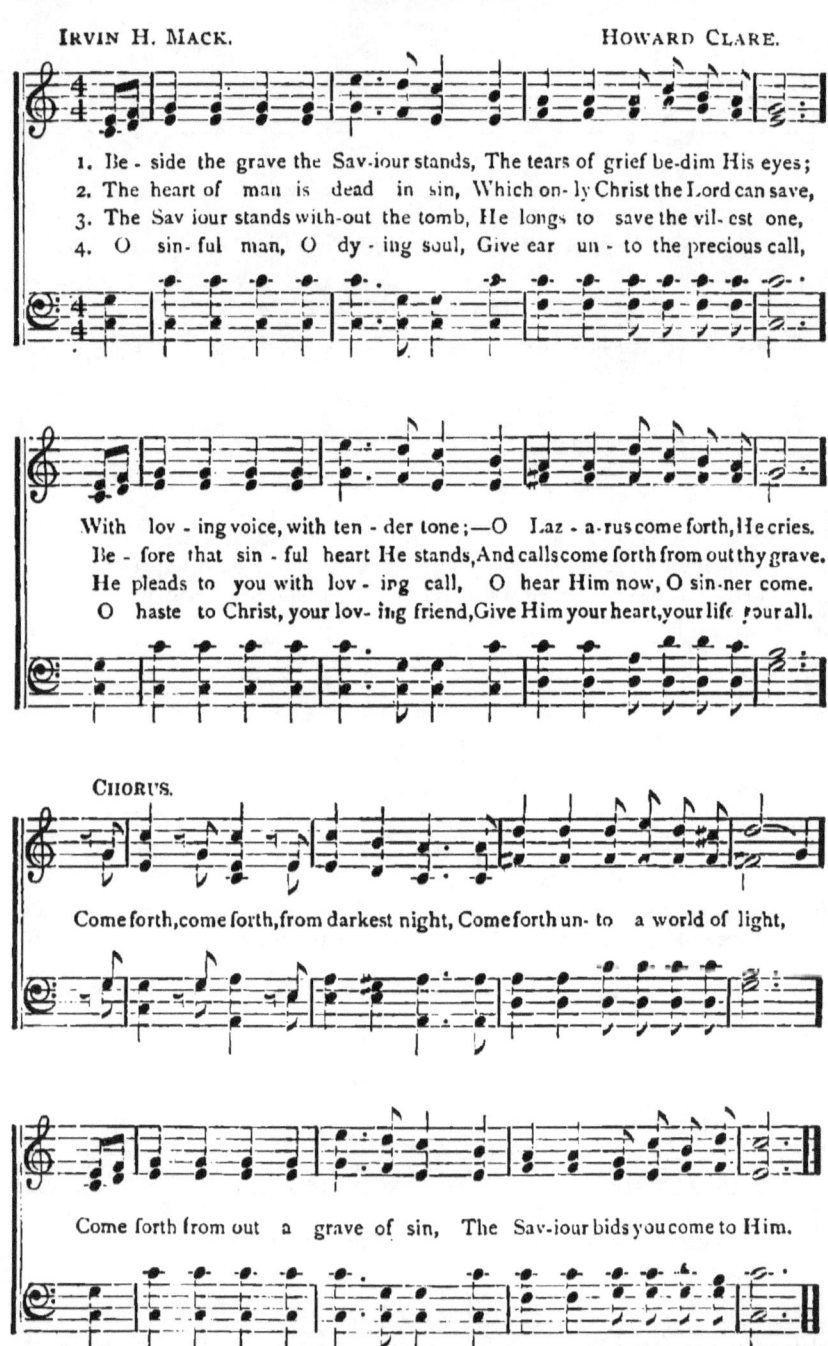

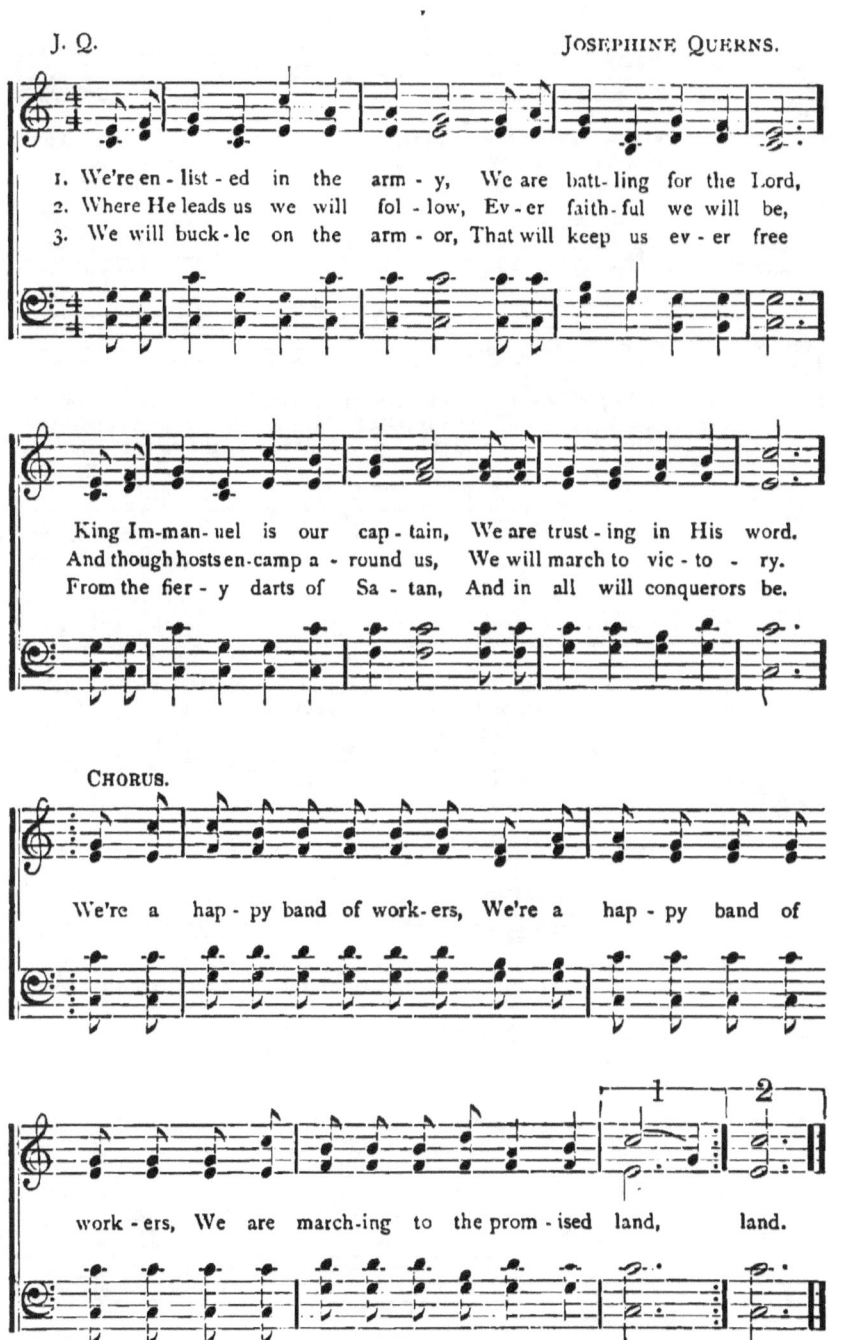

138. THE BLESSINGS OF THE LORD.

Words and Music by CHAS. BENTLEY.

1. Let us now en-joy the blessings of the Lord, who freely gives, And for-ever claim the promise with de-light; Sac-ri-fice the worldly pleasures, and for-ever near Him live, In the ser-vice of the Master and the right.
2. Lead us Lord that we may guide the wand'rers to thy blessed feet, And to bear the cross with patience all the way; Gladly give us willing hearts to praise thee at thy mer-cy seat, With the knowledge of Thy Spir-it ev-'ry day.
3. Let us glad-ly bear the tri-als as the journey we pur-sue, In the sunlight, shades, and storms of ev'ry kind; Let us lis-ten to the voice of Him who gent-ly bids us do, Leave a world of sin-ful pleasure far be-hind.

CHO.—*faith, believe His promise and His face we soon shall see, Hal-le-lu-jah! hal-le-lu-jah! I am saved.*

CHORUS.

Let us now . . . . . en-joy the bless - - ings,
Let us now en-joy the bless-ings, yes just now
of the Lord . . . . who free-ly gives; Now have
of the Lord who free-ly gives, free-ly gives;

Copyright, 1895, by Chas. Bentley.

CHILDREN OF THE EARTH, REJOICE. Concluded.

HOSANNA, BE THE CHILDREN'S SONG.

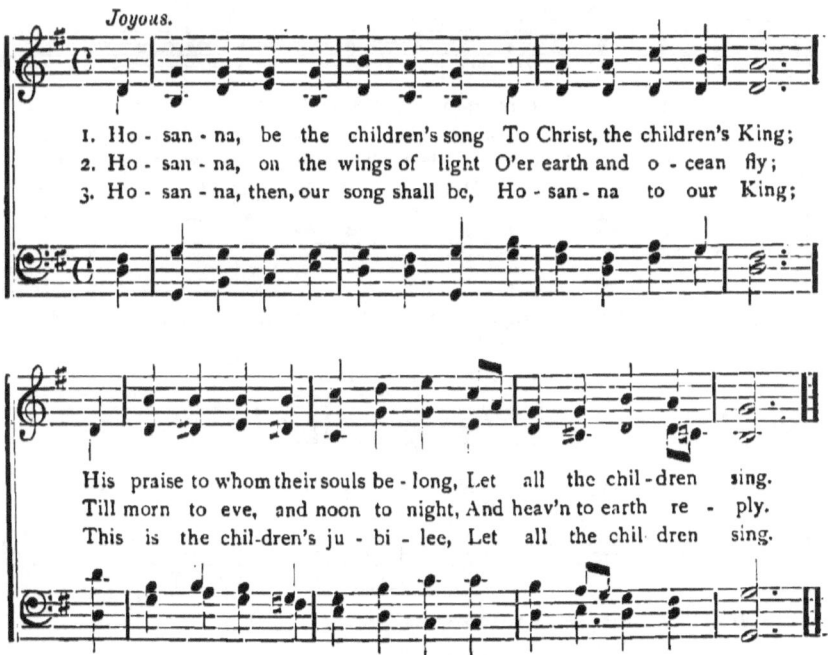

SAVED EVEN NOW. Concluded.

meet, 'twas to meet, My dear Sav-iour when I made the sol-emn vow, solemn vow,

ABIDE WITH ME!

HENRY F. LYTE.   WILLIAM HENRY MONK.

1. A - bide with me! fast falls the e - ven - tide, The dark-ness deep - ens— Lord, with me a - bide! When oth - er help - ers fail, and com-forts flee, Help of the help-less, O a - bide with me!
2. Swift to its close ebbs out life's lit - tle day; Earth's joys grow dim, its glo - ries pass a - way; Change and de - cay in all a - round I see; O Thou, who changest not, a - bide with me!
3. I need Thy pres - ence ev - 'ry pass-ing hour; What but Thy grace can foil the temp-ter's pow'r? Who, like Thy - self, my guide and stay can be? Through cloud and sunshine, Lord, a - bide with me!
4. I fear no foe, with Thee at hand to bless; Ills have no weight, and tears no bit - ter - ness; Where is death's sting? where, grave, thy vic - to - ry? I tri - umph still, if Thou a - bide with me!
5. Hold Thou Thy cross be - fore my clos- ing eyes; Shine through the gloom and point me to the skies; Heav'ns morn-ing breaks, and earth's vain shadows flee; In life, in death, O Lord, a - bide with me!

THERE IS JOY. Concluded.

I am safe what-'er be-tide, Yes with Je-sus ev-er near me there is joy.

SAVED TO SERVE.

Rev. S. W. Cope.   FRANK M. DAVIS, by per.
Moderato.

1. Yes saved to serve, I watch and pray, And stand re-joic-ing ev-'ry day,
2. Yes saved to serve, I share my store, To clothe and feed the hum-ble poor,
3. Yes saved to serve, I toil and strive, O Lord my God, Thy work re-vive,

Would love the Lord with all my heart, And from His pre-cepts ne'er de-part.
And send the gos-pel all a-broad, In hon-or of the Lord my God.
Thy king-dom come, Thy will be done, From ris-ing to the set-ting sun.

REFRAIN.

Yes saved to serve by faith I live, To God my time and tal-ents give,
Yes saved to serve Lord I am Thine, On fire of love a light to shine,
Yes saved to serve O Lord we meet, And pay our hom-age at Thy feet,

I seek to know His grac-ious will, And all His law of love ful-fill.
To oth-ers show the nar-row way, That leads to joy of end-less day.
Thy name and ma-jes-ty a-dore, We'll love and serve Thee ev-er-more.

Copyright, 1896, by Frank M. Davis.

SHOUT THE SAVIOUR'S PRAISES. Concluded. 147

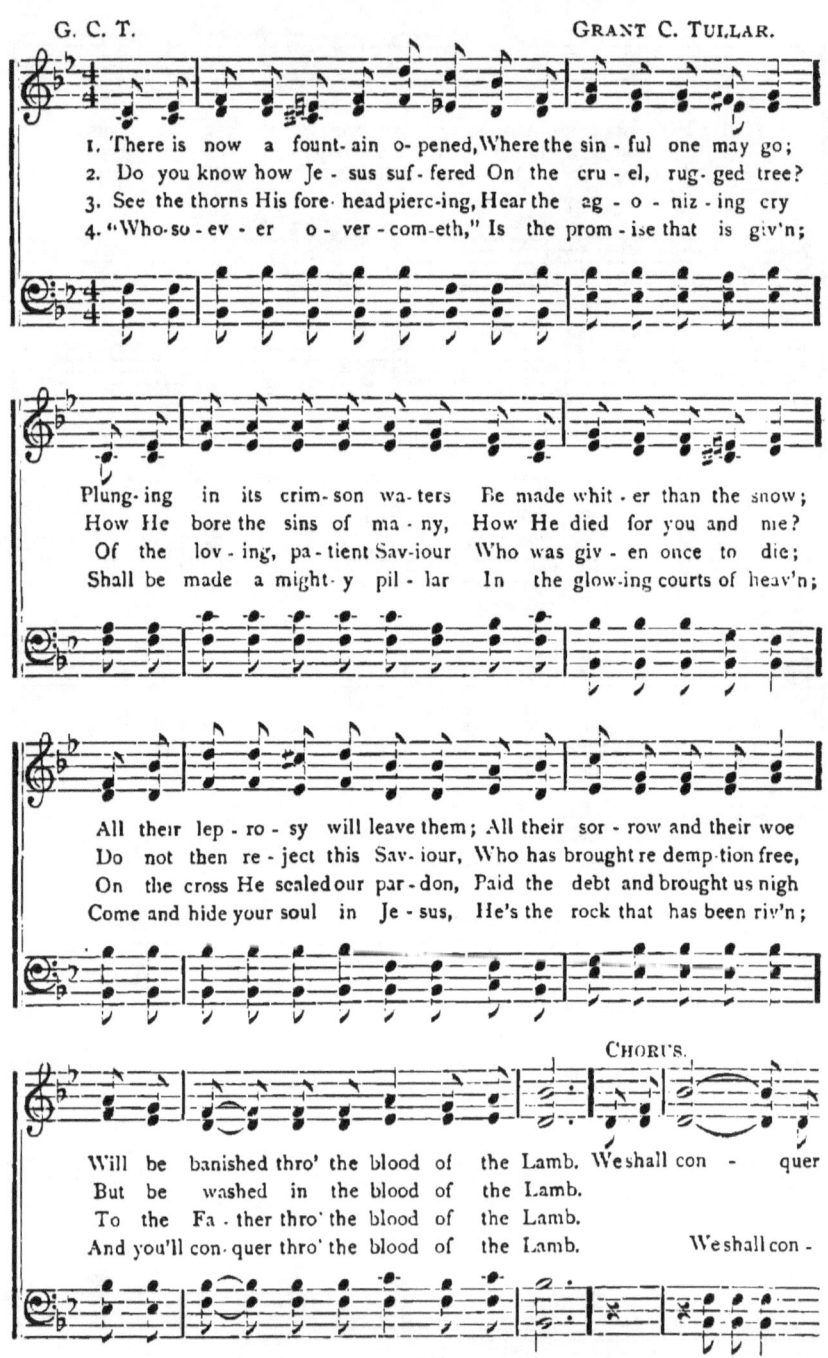

CONQUER THROUGH THE BLOOD. Concluded.

MY SOUL, BE ON THY GUARD.

GEO. E. HEATH. Dr. LOWELL MASON.

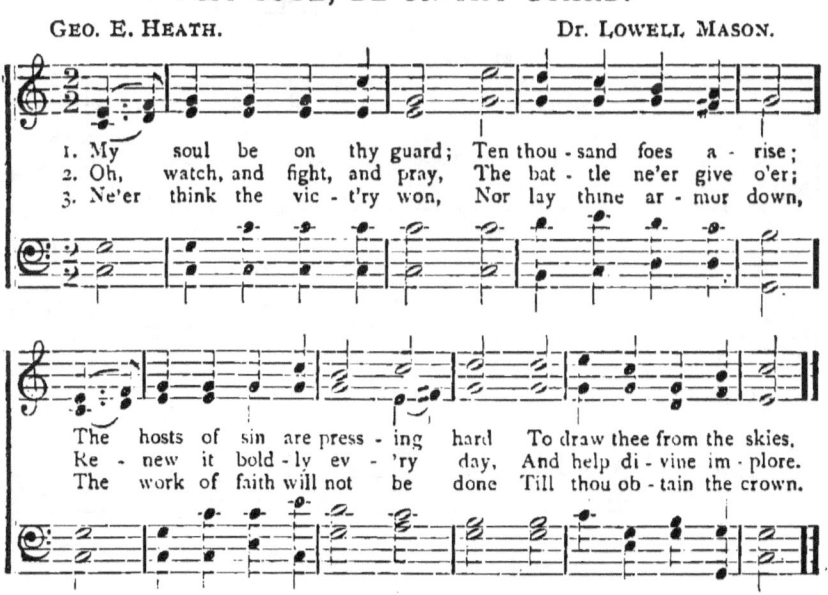

CHRIST'S SACRIFICE.—Concluded.

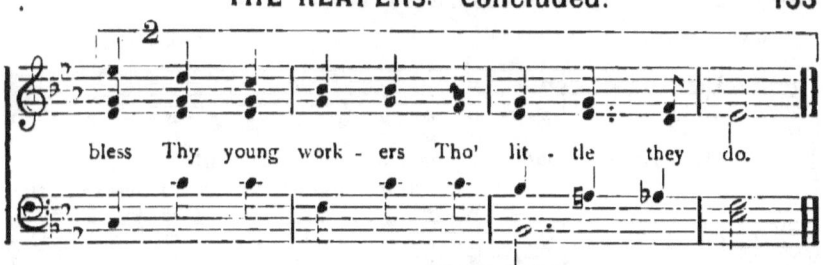

IN MY SAVIOUR'S CARE.

P. A. H.
Philip A. Hall.

1. I am rest-ing, sweetly rest-ing, I am safe from all a-larm,
2. I am trust-ing, dai-ly trust-ing, In my Sav-iour's pow'r to keep;
3. I am hop-ing, ev-er hop-ing, When my Sav-iour comes to reign,
4. Let us al-ways then be read-y For the com-ing of the King;

In the arms of my Re-deem-er; He'll pro-tect me from all harm.
In my wak-ing hours He'll guide me, And pro-tect me while a-sleep.
I will be a-mong the ran-somed, Sav'd for-ev-er from sin's stain.
Then we'll crown the bless-ed Je-sus, And His prais-es ev-er sing.

CHORUS.

I am rest-ing, I am trust-ing, I am in my Saviour's care;
At the cross I am a-bid-ing, I am safe for-ev-er there.

Copyright, 1896, by Hall-Mack Co.

THE MASTER IS WATCHING. Concluded. 155

wait-ing that they could not see; They were not darker in their lonely lot, They were not blind-er than at times are we.

  2 Oh! blessed feet that pressed the sandy beach,
   Oh! blessed hands, so willing still to save,
   No toiling one can drift beyond thy reach,
   No trusting one will sink beneath the wave.

For Alto, Tenor, and Bass.
  2 Oh! blessed feet that pressed the beach, the sandy beach,
   Oh! blessed, blessed hands, so willing still to save,
   No toiling one can drift, can drift beyond thy reach,
   No trusting one will sink, will sink beneath the wave.

  3 The angry billows knew their Master first,
   And bore his weight upon their foamy crest;
   Is Nature keener, or is man the worst,
   That they were slow to greet the Heavenly Guest?

For Alto, Tenor, and Bass.
  3 The angry billows knew him first, their Master first,
   And bore his weight upon their crest, their foamy crest;
   Is Nature keener, or is man, is man the worst,
   That they were slow, were slow to greet the Heavenly Guest.

  4 No ship can sink when he is at the helm,
   No craft can founder on life's stormy tide,
   No sea engulf or angry wave o'erwhelm,
   When he who forms the waves is at our side.

For Alto, Tenor, and Bass.
  4 No ship, no ship can sink while he is at the helm,
   No craft, no craft can founder on life's stormy tide,
   No sea, no sea engulf or angry wave o'erwhelm,
   When he, when he who forms the waves is at our side.

ONLY THINE, PRECIOUS LORD. 161

PEMBERTON PIERCE.   R. J. SHOEMAKER.

1. I would be thine, most holy Lord, Oh, fill my heart with love divine,
2. Ah, yes, to thee I fain would live, To thee, who for my ransom died;

And teach me from thy precious word, That I may yet still brighter shine.
Teach me to pray, that I may give My life and all I have beside.

CHORUS.

Make me thine, yes, thine, Thine alone, precious Lord, would I be;
make me thine, ever thine,

Make me thine, on-ly thine, Dear Lord, remember me.
make me thine, only thine,

3 Thy sinless mind in me reveal,
   Thy nature to my soul impart,
   And all my future life shall tell
     The fulness of a loving heart.

4 Then fill my soul with holy fire,
   Thou sacred spirit, from above;
   Make all ablaze with pure desire;
     Expand my heart with heavenly love.

Copyright, 1880.
From "Rays of Sunshine." Used by per.

IN JESUS. Concluded. 163

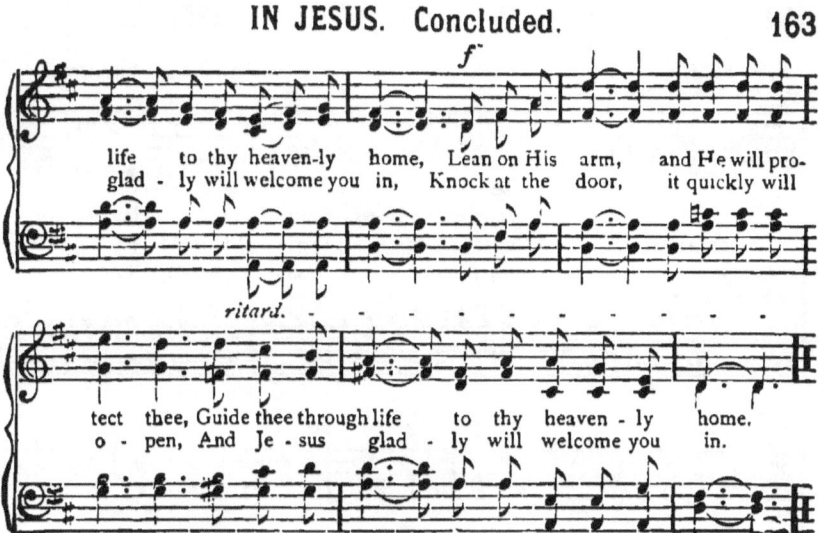

3 Resting in Jesus, resting in Jesus,
   He is my Guide, my Shepherd my Life;
   Resting in Jesus, resting in Jesus,
   You who would rest from your trouble and strife,
   Flee to Him now, and He will receive you,
   Rest in his love, and your guide He will be,
   Peace He will give to all who will ask it,
   Come to Him now, for His mercy is free.

WEBER. 7s.

Rev. CHAS. WESLEY.   C. M. VON WEBER.

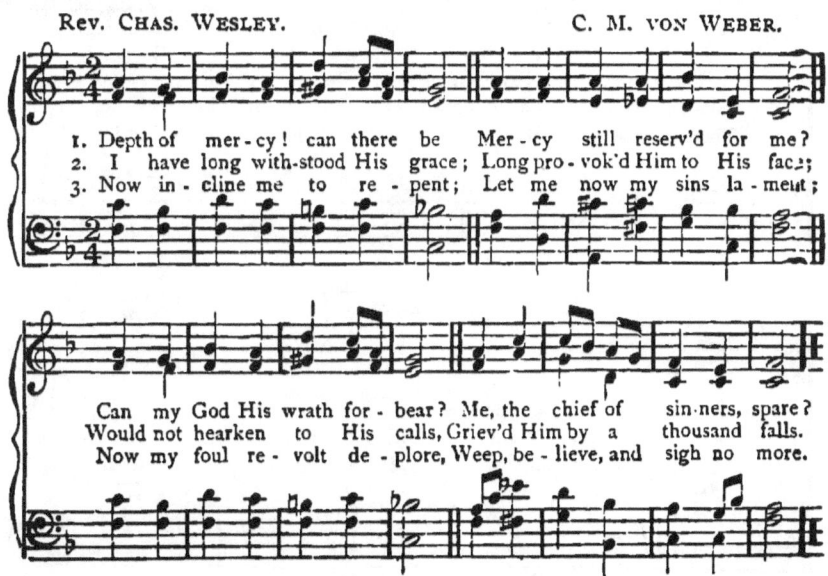

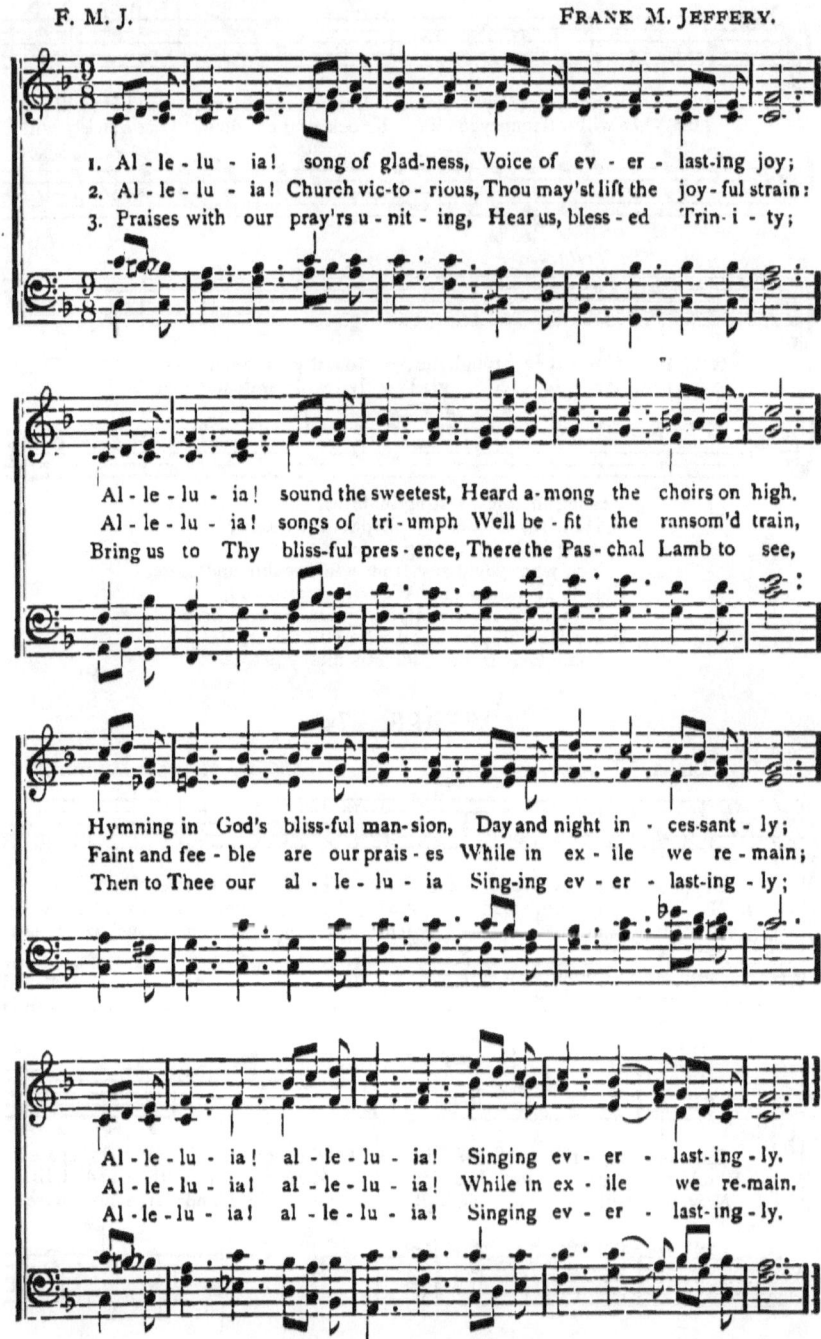

168 YOUR INFLUENCE.

LAURA E. NEWELL.   ADAM GEIBEL.
Solo or Quartette.
With expression, not too slowly.

1. O! what shall your in-flu-ence be? . . . Will it el-e-vate, strength-en and bless? Shall each one who meets you dis-cov-er A friend in this world's wil-der-ness? Will the weak be in-spir'd by your pres-ence?
2. Will you work with un-wav'-ring pur-pose, . . . At the duties that fall to your lot, Do-ing earn-est-ly, faith-ful-ly, no-bly? Your ac-tions will not be for-got. Will you reap in life's vine-yard much fruit-age,
3. Or will you be aim-less and sloth-ful, . . . Nor care for the ones by the way, On-ly think-ing of self and not reck'-ning, If ma-ny a-round you should stray? Not off'-ring a word, kind-ly spo-ken,
4. Let each one but help some weak broth-er, . . . We need not go far to do good, But with will-ing hands help one an-oth-er, We all might do much if we would; And the Fa-ther will lend us as-sist-ance

Copyrighted in "The Helper." Used by per.

170 ONWARD, CHRISTIAN SOLDIERS.

Rev. S. Baring Gould.   Frank M. Jeffery.

1. On-ward, Christian sol - diers, March-ing as to war,
2. Like a might-y ar - my, Moves the Church of God:
3. Crowns and thrones may per - ish, King doms rise and wane,
4. On-ward, then, ye faith - ful, Join our hap-py throng,

With the cross of Je - sus Go-ing on be-fore.
Broth-ers, we are tread - ing Where the saints have trod.
But the Church of Je - sus Con-stant will re-main,
Blend with ours your voic - es, In the tri-umph-song:

Christ, the roy - al Mas - ter, Leads a-gainst the foe;
We are not di - vi - ded, All one bod - y we,
Gates of hell can nev - er 'Gainst that church pre - vail:
Glo - ry, laud, and hon - or, Un - to Christ the King:

For-ward in - to bat - tle, See, His ban - ners go.
One in hope and doc - trine, One in char - i - ty.
We have Christ's own prom - ise, And that can - not fail.
This, thro' countless a - ges, Men and an - gels sing,

Copyright, 1896, by Frank M. Jeffery.

ONWARD, CHRISTIAN SOLDIERS. Concluded. 171

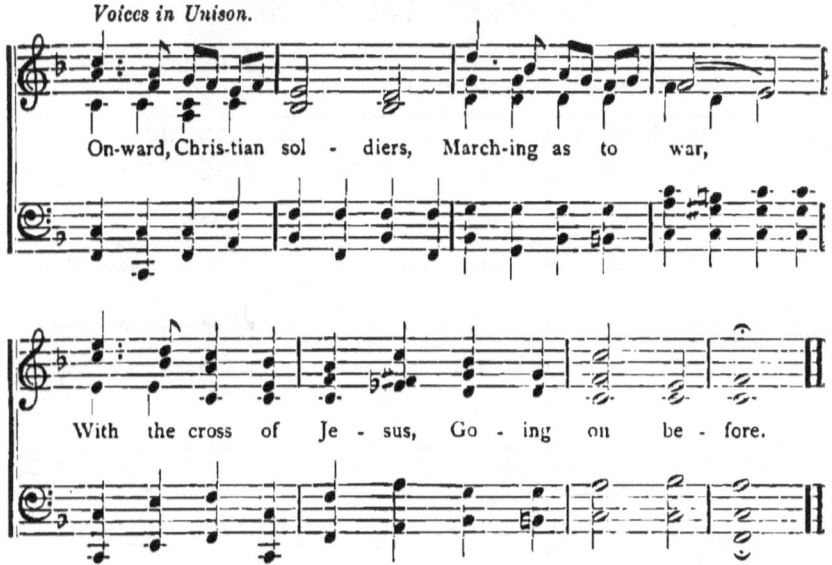

On-ward, Chris-tian sol - diers, March-ing as to war,
With the cross of Je - sus, Go - ing on be - fore.

JESUS! NAME OF WONDROUS LOVE!

L. M. GOTTSCHALK.

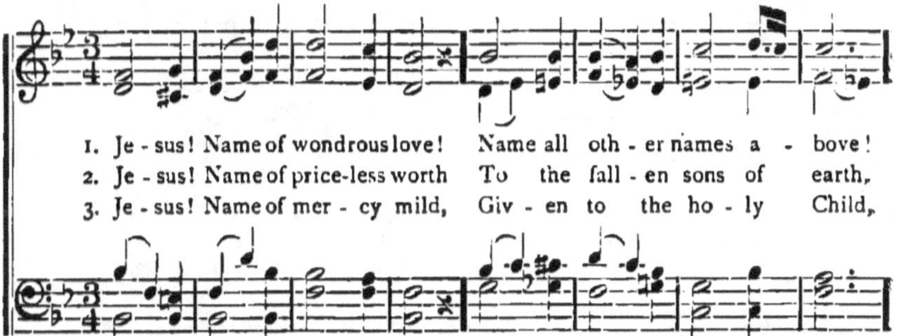

1. Je - sus! Name of wondrous love! Name all oth - er names a - bove!
2. Je - sus! Name of price-less worth To the fall - en sons of earth,
3. Je - sus! Name of mer - cy mild, Giv - en to the ho - ly Child,

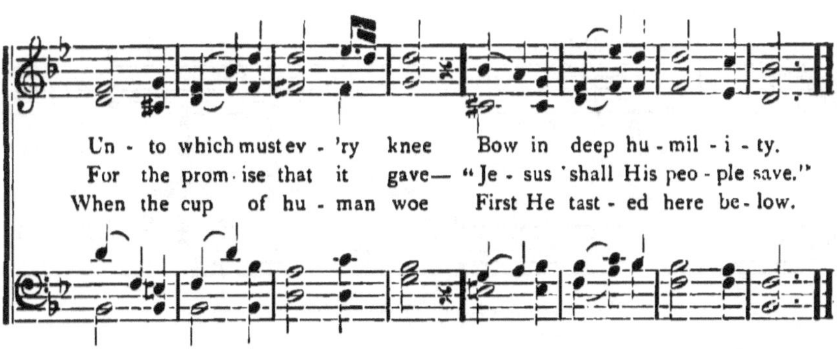

Un - to which must ev - 'ry knee Bow in deep hu - mil - i - ty.
For the prom - ise that it gave— "Je - sus shall His peo - ple save."
When the cup of hu - man woe First He tast - ed here be - low.

172

JERUSALEM, THE GRAND.

HARRY MACK. J. LINCOLN HALL.
(Verse may be sung as a Quartette.)

1. Je - ru - sa - lem, the grand,... The rich re - splen - dent goal;... Je - ru - sa - lem, the prom - ised land, A - waits the loy - al soul....
2. The na - tions of the saved,... The low - ly and the king,... Shall tread the streets with rich - es paved, And songs of free - dom sing....
3. On earth they need the sun,... To guide their steps a - right;... In heav - en, Christ, the Ho - ly One Sheds forth trans - cend - ent light....

CHORUS. (UNISON.)

And they shall reign... for - ev - er and

Copyrighted, 1898, by Hall-Mack Co.

JERUSALEM, THE GRAND.—Concluded.

When I Reach the Gates of Glory. Concluded. 175

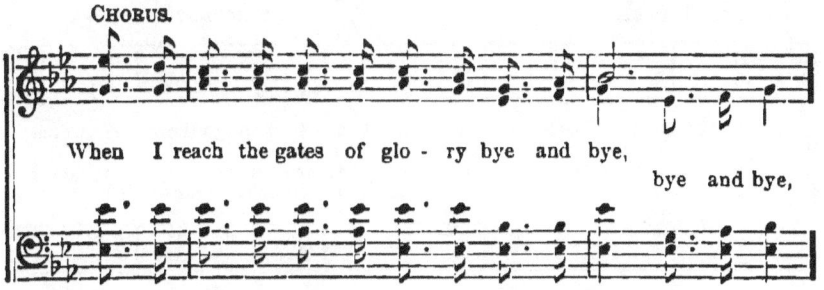

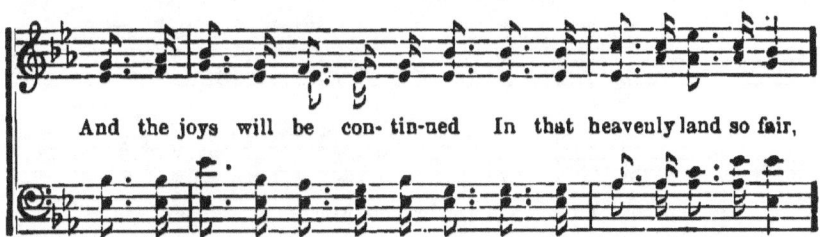
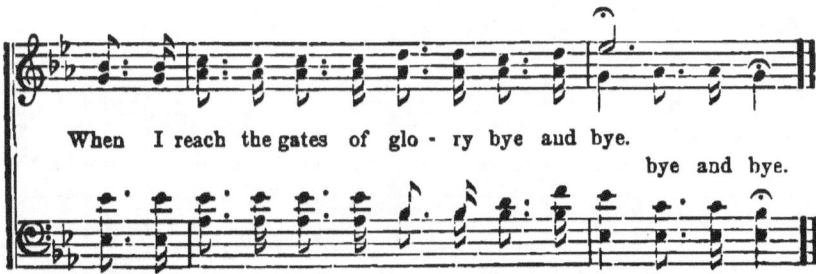

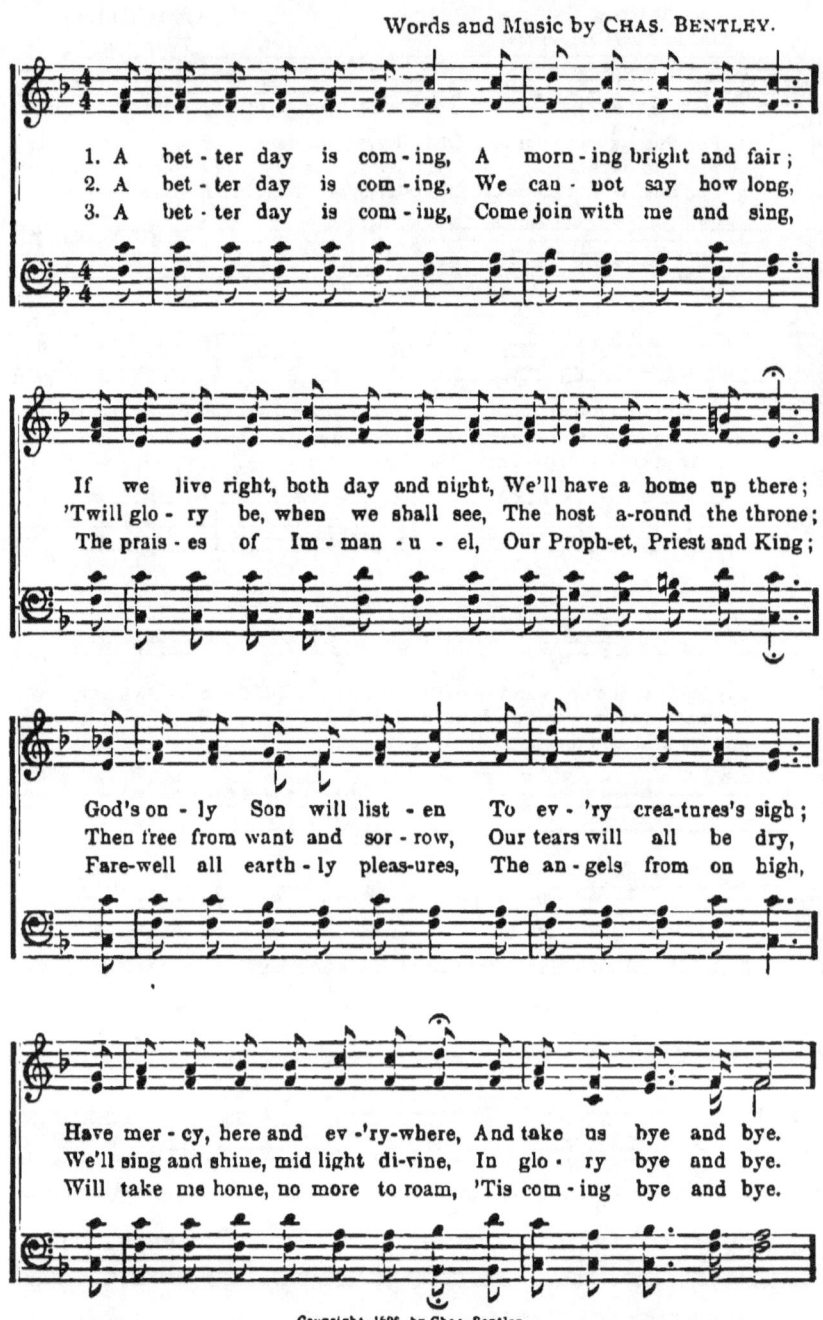

COMING BYE AND BYE. Concluded. 179

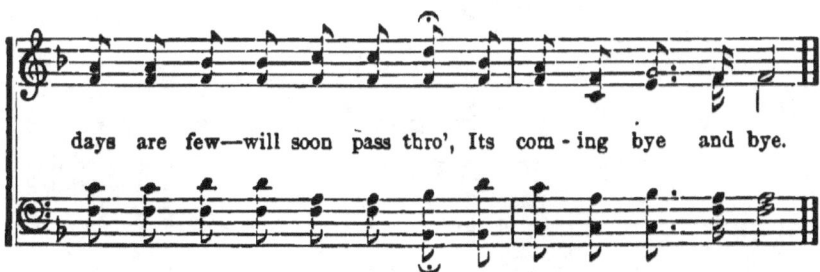

BLESSED SAVIOUR.

GEO. M. VICKERS. ADAM GEIBEL.

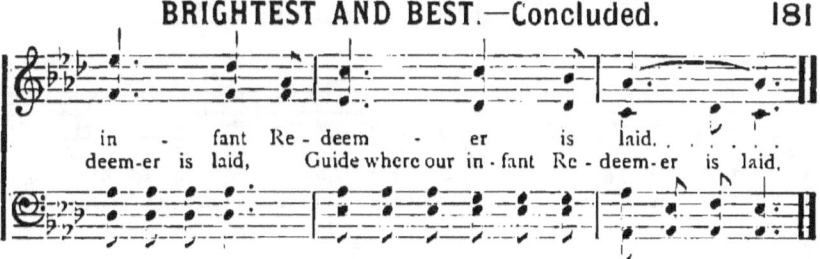

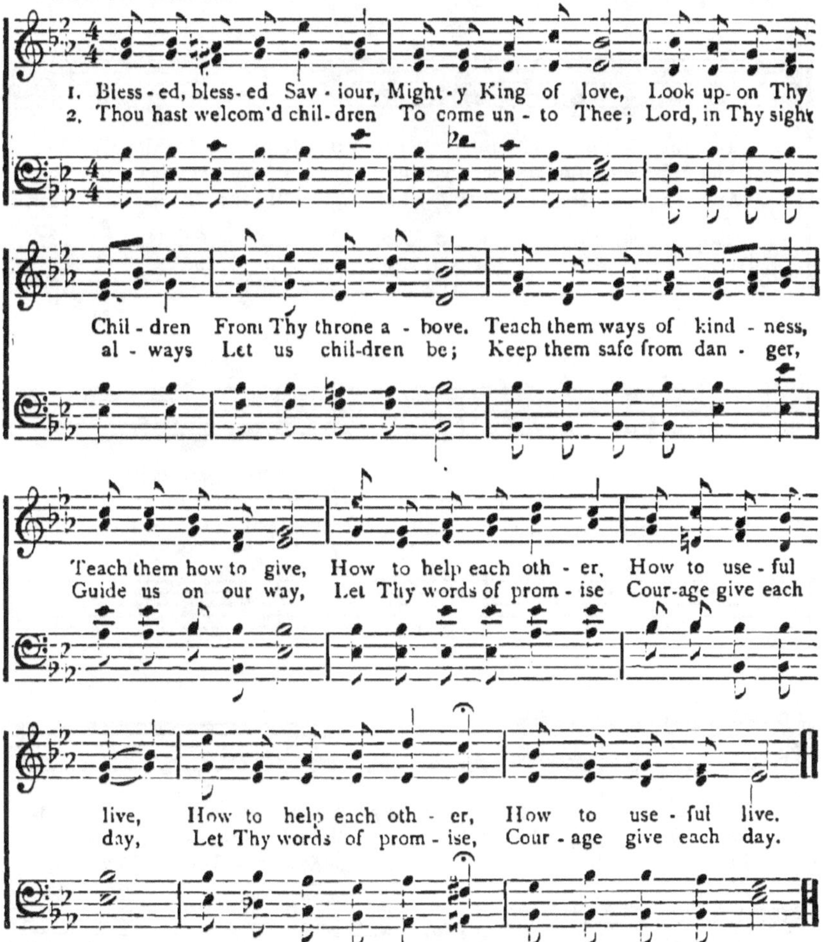

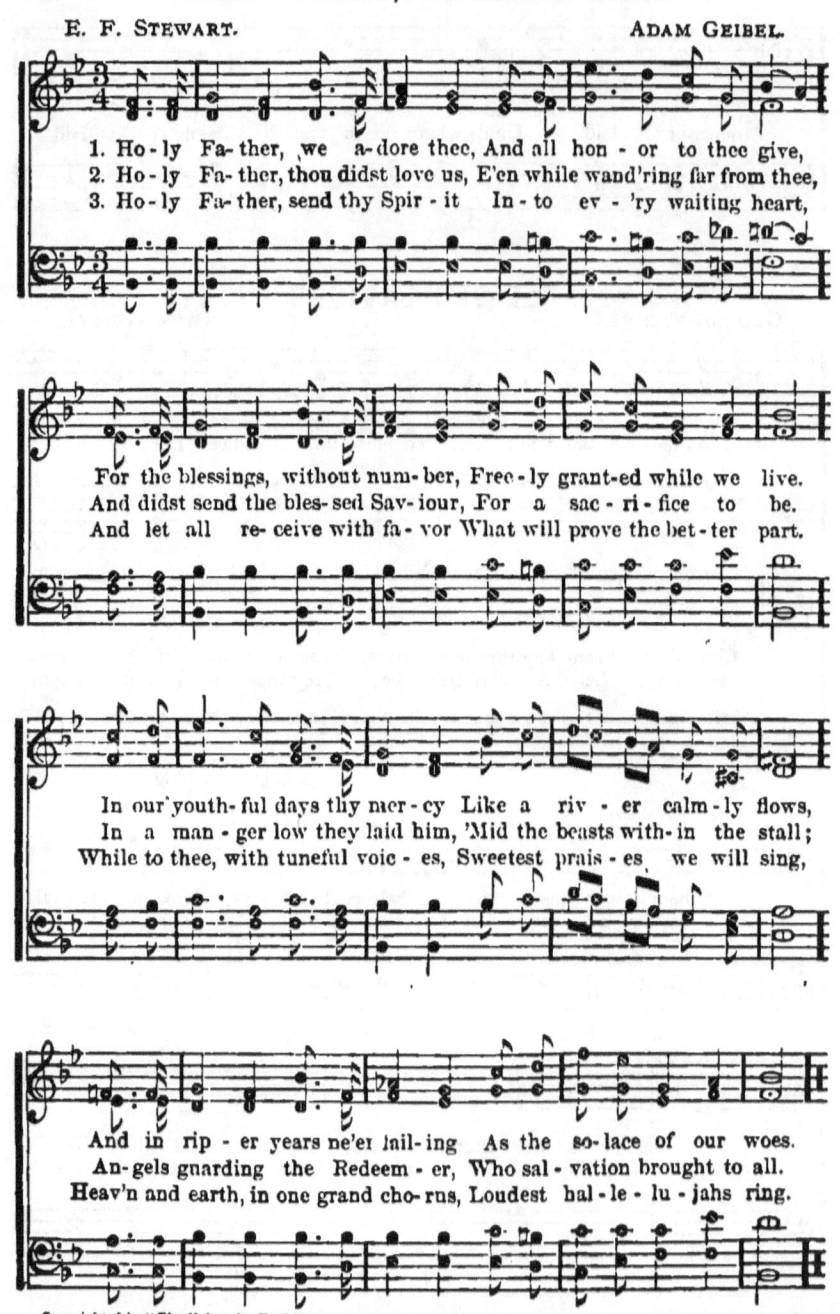

BETHESDA. Concluded. 185

Refrain. Quartette.

TRUSTING.

P. P.   Pemberton Pierce.

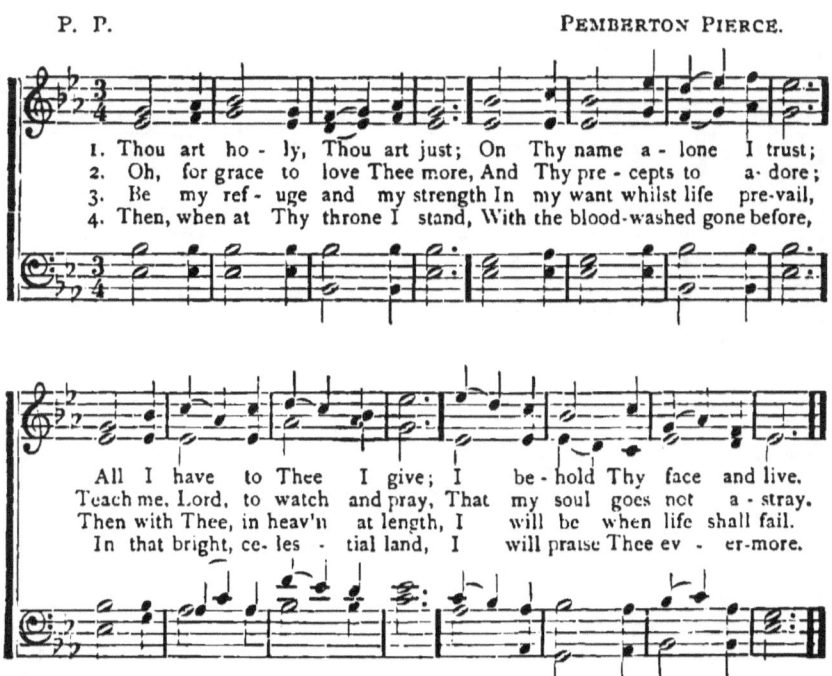

1. Thou art ho-ly, Thou art just; On Thy name a-lone I trust;
2. Oh, for grace to love Thee more, And Thy pre-cepts to a-dore;
3. Be my ref-uge and my strength In my want whilst life pre-vail,
4. Then, when at Thy throne I stand, With the blood-washed gone before,

All I have to Thee I give; I be-hold Thy face and live.
Teach me, Lord, to watch and pray, That my soul goes not a-stray.
Then with Thee, in heav'n at length, I will be when life shall fail.
In that bright, ce-les-tial land, I will praise Thee ev-er-more.

Copyrighted in "The Helper." Used by per.

186 ARE WE MAKING THE MOST OF OUR MOMENTS?

LAURA E. NEWELL.   PEMBERTON PIERCE.

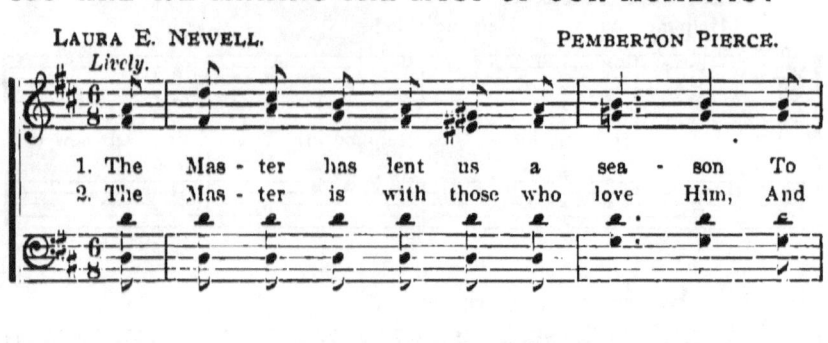

1. The Mas-ter has lent us a sea-son To
2. The Mas-ter is with those who love Him, And

live and o-bey His com-mands; The fields are all
guides them with ten-der-est hand To fields that are

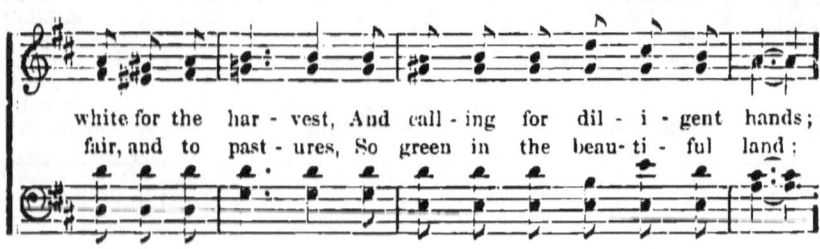

white for the har-vest, And call-ing for dil-i-gent hands;
fair, and to past-ures, So green in the beau-ti-ful land;

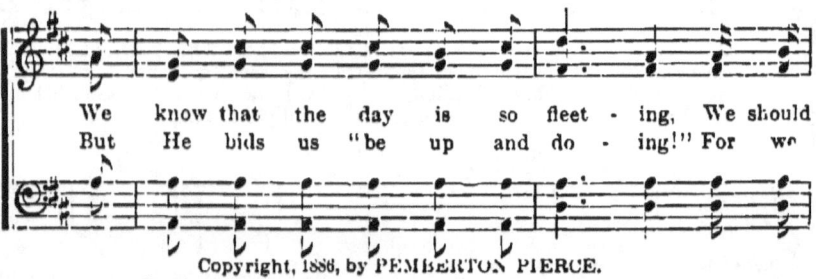

We know that the day is so fleet-ing, We should
But He bids us "be up and do-ing!" For we

Copyright, 1886, by PEMBERTON PIERCE.

From "Rays of Sunshine." Used by per.

WHEN HIS SALVATION BRINGING. 189

JOHN KING.
FRANK M. JEFFERY.

1. When His sal-va-tion bring-ing, To Zi-on Jesus came,
2. And since the Lord re-tain-eth, His love to chil-dren still,
3. For should we fail pro-claim-ing, Our great Re-deem-er's praise,

The chil-dren all stood sing-ing, Ho-san-na to His name;
Though now as King He reign-eth On Zi-on's heav'n-ly hill;
The stones, our si-lence sham-ing, Might well ho-san-nas raise;

Nor did their zeal of-fend Him, But as He rode a-long,
We'll flock a-round His ban-ner, Who sits up-on the throne,
But shall we on-ly ren-der, The trib-ute of our words?

He let them still at-tend Him, And smiled to hear their song.
And cry a-loud, Ho-san-na, To Da-vid's roy-al Son.
No, while our hearts are ten-der, They too shall be the Lord's.

CHORUS. *in Unison.*

Ho-san-na, Ho-san-na, To Je-sus they sang.
Ho-san-na, Ho-san-na, To Je-sus we'll sing.
Ho-san-na, Ho-san-na, To Je-sus our King.

Copyright, 1896, by Frank M. Jeffery.

Oh, the Pure Cleansing Fountain. Concluded. 193

3 I will publish to all the glad news of salvation;
   Thy wonderful mercy my heart shall indite;
   O refuge, so mighty! O help, that is cheering!
   For the hour that is darkest Thy love is the light.

SING UNTO JESUS.—Concluded.

200 EVERY HOUR I NEED THY BLESSING.

ELIZABETH J. T.   WILL L. THOMPSON.

Slowly.

1. Ev-'ry hour I need Thy bless-ing, Ev-'ry mo-ment need Thy care,
2. Ev-'ry hour I need Thy bless-ing, Dai-ly need Thy wondrous love,
3. Ev-'ry hour I need Thy bless-ing, Ev-'ry mo-ment need Thy care,

Lord, to Thee I come con-fess-ing, All the sins that me en-snare.
Love so ten-der, so pro-tect-ing, Coming from Thy throne a-bove.
Un-til Thou my soul pos-sess-ing, Shall re-flect Thine im-age there.

Bless the thoughts that come each moment, Make them true and pure and fair,
For Thy lov-ing care and bless-ing, Make me thank-ful day by day,
Then to Christ the King of Glo-ry, He who bought me with great price,

Like to Thine our great a-tone-ment, Beau-ti-ful be-yond compare.
By my walk and dai-ly liv-ing, Prais-ing Christ the Liv-ing Way.
I shall sing the old, old sto-ry, Christ my Lord, my sac-ri-fice.

CHORUS.

Come, O come Thou lov-ing Sav-iour, Take me
Come, O come Thou lov-ing Sav-iour come,

By permission of Will L. Thompson & Co., East Liverpool, Ohio.

Every Hour I Need Thy Blessing. Concluded. 201

in Thy ten-der care, Watch and guide me ev-'ry
Take me in Thy ten-der care, Watch and guide me

mo-ment, And my soul for Thee pre-pare.
ev-'ry mo-ment, come, And my soul for Thee pre-pare.

MY SPIRIT ON THY CARE.

H. W. GREATOREX.

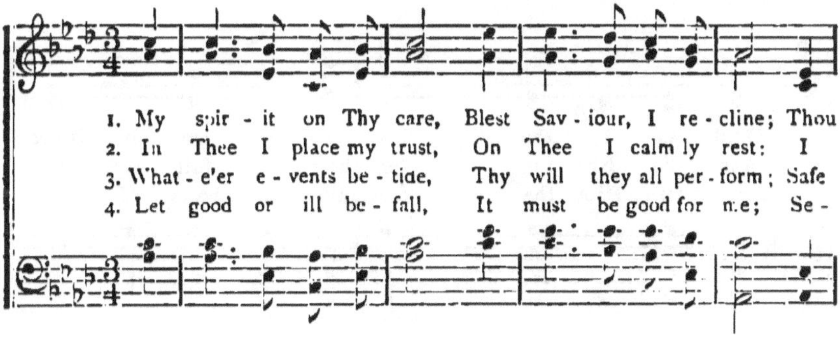

1. My spir-it on Thy care, Blest Sav-iour, I re-cline; Thou
2. In Thee I place my trust, On Thee I calm-ly rest: I
3. What-e'er e-vents be-tide, Thy will they all per-form; Safe
4. Let good or ill be-fall, It must be good for me; Se-

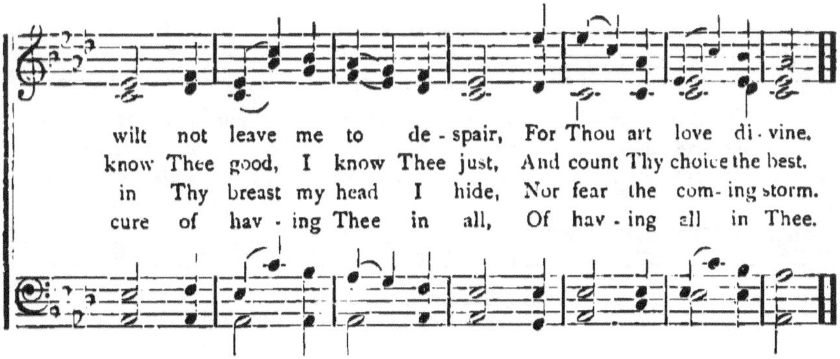

wilt not leave me to de-spair, For Thou art love di-vine.
know Thee good, I know Thee just, And count Thy choice the best.
in Thy breast my head I hide, Nor fear the com-ing storm.
cure of hav-ing Thee in all, Of hav-ing all in Thee.

A SUMMER SONG.

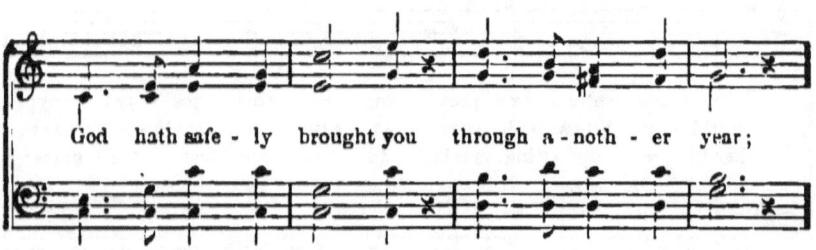

Used by per. from "The Helper."

A SUMMER SONG.—Concluded.

206 SOMEWHERE.

IRVIN H. MACK. J. LINCOLN HALL.

1. Some-where the sun is bright-ly beam-ing, Tho' tis hidden from your view,
2. Some-where the Sav-iour stands to greet you, Yon-der in a bright-er land,
3. Some-where there's life and love and glad-ness, Je-sus is not far a-way,
4. Some-where, with-out the fold you're stray-ing, Straying from the Saviour's home,
5. Some-where with in the world you're straying, In a world that's ev-er cold,

Some-where the light of hope is gleam-ing, Gleam-ing bright for you.
Some-where your loved ones long to meet you, On the Jor-dan's strand.
Some-where we'll meet, where is no sad-ness, Ev-er there to stay.
Some-where, a heart for you is pray-ing, Rest, and cease to roam.
Some-where the prec-ious step de-lay-ing, En-ter now the fold.

CHORUS. *in Unison.*

Then trust in God thro' all thy days, Fear not for He is by thy

PARTS.

side, He'll lead thee thro' life's devious ways, He will guide where no storms betide.

Copyright, 1896, by Hall-Mack Co.

BIRDS AND BLOSSOMS.

Words and Music by Rev. ARTHUR W. SPOONER.

WE WILL GO TO SUNDAY SCHOOL.

Words and Music furnished by Rev. Dr. WM. SWINDELLS.

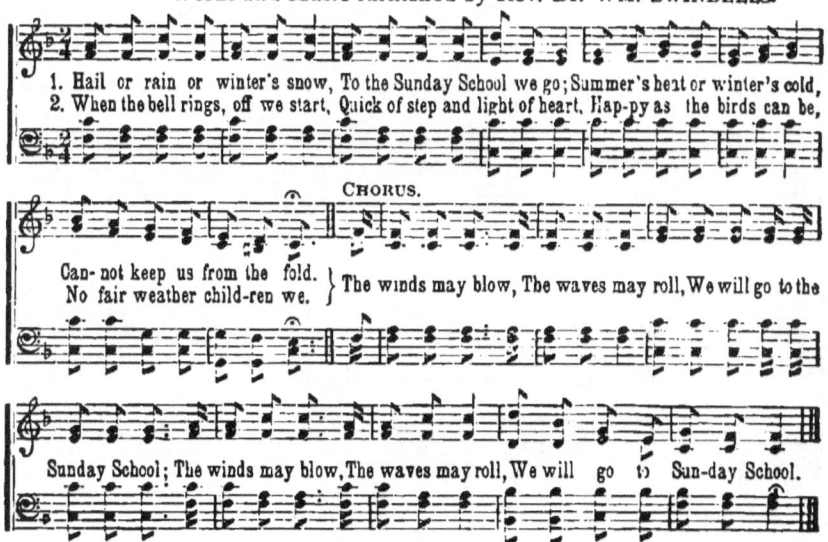

Copyrighted, 1896, by Hall-Mack Co.

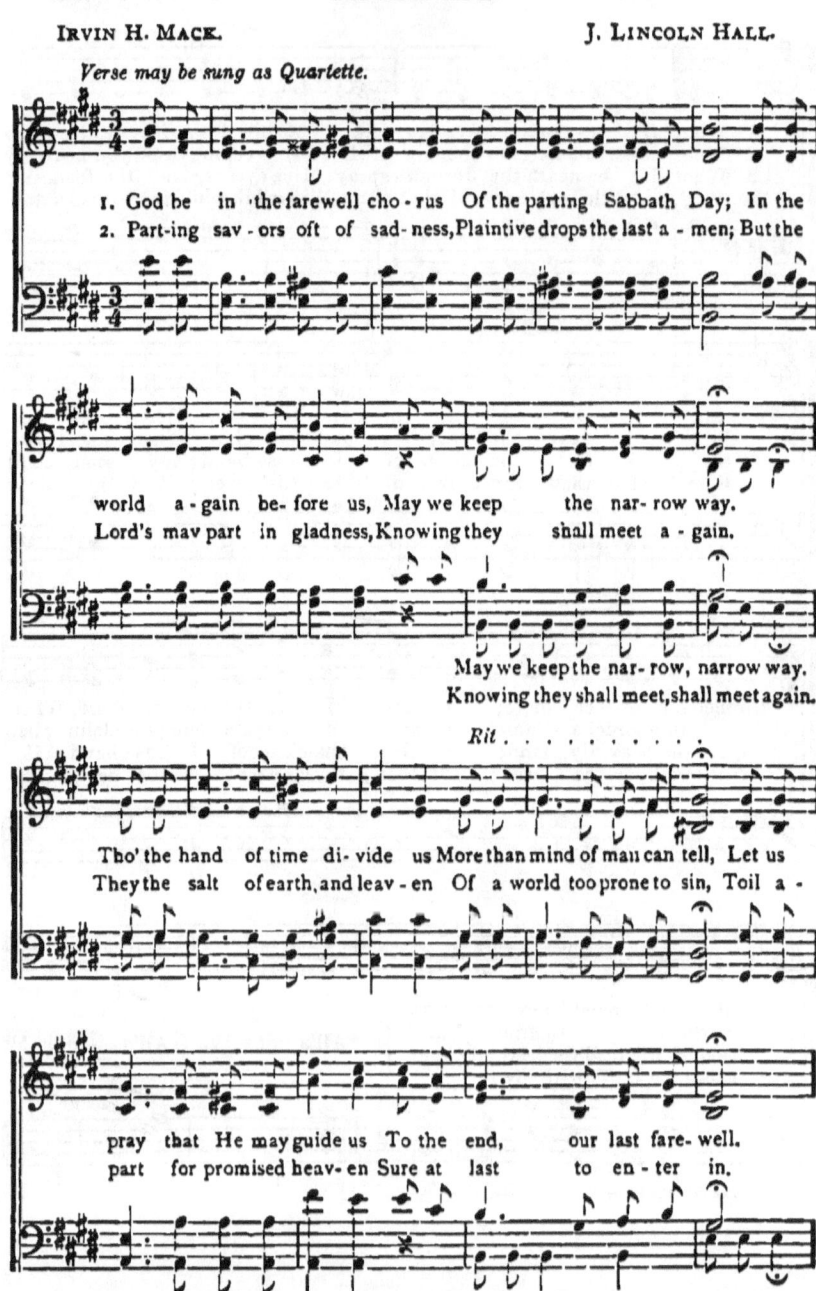

A SONG OF SPRING.—Concluded.

217

STAND UP FOR JESUS.

1 Stand up, stand up for Jesus,
    Ye soldiers of the cross;
  Lift high His royal banner,
    It must not suffer loss:
  From victory unto victory
    His army shall He lead,
  Till every foe is vanquished
    And Christ is Lord indeed.

2 Stand up, stand up for Jesus,
    The trumpet call obey;
  Forth to the mighty conflict,
    In this His glorious day:
  "Ye that are men, now serve Him,"
    Against unnumbered foes;
  Your courage rise with danger,
    And strength to strength oppose.

JUST AS I AM.

1 Just as I am, without one plea,
  But that Thy blood was shed for me,
  And that Thou bid'st me come to Thee,
    O Lamb of God, I come!

2 Just as I am, and waiting not
  To rid my soul of one dark blot,
  To Thee, whose blood can cleanse each
    O Lamb of God, I come!   [spot,

3 Just as I am—Thou wilt receive,
  Wilt welcome, pardon, cleanse, relieve;
  Because Thy promise I believe,
    O Lamb of God, I come!

4 Just as I am—Thy love unknown
  Hath broken every barrier down;
  Now, to be Thine, yea, thine alone,
    O Lamb of God, I come!

WORK FOR THE NIGHT IS COMING.

1 Work for the night is coming,
    Work through the morning hours;
  Work, while the dew is sparkling,
    Work 'mid springing flowers;
  Work, when the day grows brighter,
    Work in the glowing sun;
  Work, for the night is coming,
    When man's work is done.

2 Work, for the night is coming,
    Work through the sunny noon;
  Fill brightest hours with labor,
    Rest comes sure and soon.
  Give every flying minute
    Something to keep in store;
  Work, for the night is coming,
    When man works no more.

HE LEADETH ME.

1 He leadeth me! oh, blessed thought,
  Oh, words, with heavenly comfort fraught!
  Whate'er I do, where'er I be,
  Still 'tis God's hand that leadeth me!

2 Sometimes 'mid scenes of deepest gloom,
  Sometimes where Eden's bowers bloom,
  By waters still, o'er troubled sea—
  Still 'tis His hand that leadeth me.

3 Lord, I would clasp Thy hand in mine,
  Nor ever murmur nor repine—
  Content, whatever lot I see,
  Since 'tis my God that leadeth me.

4 And when my task on earth is done,
  When, by Thy grace the victory's won,
  E'en death's cold wave I will not flee,
  Since God through Jordan leadeth me.

THE MORNING LIGHT.

1 The morning light is breaking
    The darkness disappears;
  The sons of men are waking
    To penitential tears;
  Each breeze that sweeps the ocean
    Brings tidings from afar
  Of nations in commotion,
    Prepared for Zion's war.

2 See heathen nations bending
    Before the God we love,
  And thousand hearts ascending
    In gratitude above;
  While sinners, now confessing,
    The gospel call obey,
  And seek the Saviour's blessing,
    A nation in a day.

3 Blest river of salvation,
    Pursue thine onward way;
  Flow thou to every nation,
    Nor in thy richness stay,
  Stay not till all the lowly
    Triumphant reach their home
  Stay not till all the holy
    Proclaim, "The Lord is come!"

I HEAR THY WELCOME VOICE.

1 I hear thy welcome voice,
That calls me, Lord, to Thee,
For cleansing in Thy precious blood
That flowed on Calvary.

CHORUS.

I am coming, Lord.
Coming now to Thee!
Wash me, cleanse me in the blood
That flowed on Calvary.

2 Though coming weak and vile,
Thou dost my strength assure;
Thou dost my vileness fully cleanse,
Till spotless all and pure.

3 'Tis Jesus calls me on
To perfect faith and love,
To perfect hope, and peace, and trust,
For earth and heaven above.

4 All hail, atoning blood!
All hail, redeeming grace!
All hail, the gift of Christ our Lord,
Our Strength and Righteousness!

SWEET HOUR OF PRAYER.

1 Sweet hour of prayer, sweet hour of prayer,
That calls me from a world of care,
And bids me at my Father's throne
Make all my wants and wishes known!
In seasons of distress and grief
My soul has often found relief,
And oft escaped the tempter's snare
By thy return, sweet hour of prayer.

2 Sweet hour of prayer, sweet hour of prayer,
Thy wings shall my petition bear
To Him, whose truth and faithfulness
Engage the waiting soul to bless:
And since He bids me seek His face,
Believe His word, and trust His grace.
I'll cast on Him my every care,
And wait for thee, sweet hour of prayer.

MY FAITH LOOKS UP TO THEE.

1 My faith looks up to thee,
Thou Lamb of Calvary,
Saviour divine:
Now hear me while I pray,
Take all my guilt away,
O, let me from this day
Be wholly Thine.

2 May Thy rich grace impart
Strength to my fainting heart,
My zeal inspire;
As Thou hast died for me,
O, may my love to Thee
Pure, warm, and changeless be—
A living fire.

3 While life's dark maze I tread,
And griefs around me spread,
Be Thou my guide;
Bid darkness turn to day,
Wipe sorrow's tears away,
Nor let me ever stray
From Thee aside.

PRECIOUS PROMISE.

1 Precious promise God hath given
To the weary passer by,
On the way from earth to heaven,
"I will guide thee with Mine eye."

REFRAIN.

I will guide thee, I will guide thee,
I will guide thee with Mine eye;
On the way from earth to heaven,
I will guide thee with Mine eye.

2 When temptations almost win thee,
And thy trusted watchers fly,
Let this promise ring within thee,
"I will guide thee with Mine eye."

3 When thy secret hopes have perished,
In the grave of years gone by,
Let this promise still be cherished,
"I will guide thee with Mine eye."

4 When the shades of life are falling,
And the hour has come to die,
Hear thy trusty Pilot calling,
"I will guide thee with Mine eye."

O, FOR A THOUSAND TONGUES.

1 O, for a thousand tongues to sing
My great Redeemer's praise;
The glories of my God and King,
The triumphs of His grace!

2 My gracious Master and my God,
Assist me to proclaim,
To spread through all the earth abroad
The honors of Thy name.

3 Jesus! the name that charms our fears,
That bids our sorrows cease,
'Tis music in the sinner's ears,
'Tis life, and health, and peace.

4 He breaks the power of canceled sin,
He sets the prisoner free;
His blood can make the foulest clean,
His blood availed for me.

YIELD NOT TO TEMPTATION.

1 Yield not to temptation,
 For yielding is sin,
 Each victory will help you
 Some other to win ;
 Fight manfully onward,
 Dark passions subdue,
 Look ever to Jesus,
 He'll carry you through.

CHORUS.

Ask the Saviour to help you,
Comfort, strengthen, and keep you ;
He is willing to aid you,
He will carry you through.

2 Shun evil companions,
 Bad language disdain,
 God's name hold in reverence,
 Nor take it in vain :
 Be thoughtful and earnest,
 Kind-hearted and true,
 Look ever to Jesus,
 He'll carry you through.

3 To him that o'ercometh
 God giveth a crown,
 Through faith we shall conquer,
 Though often cast down ;
 He who is our Saviour,
 Our strength will renew,
 Look ever to Jesus,
 He'll carry you through.

BRINGING IN THE SHEAVES.

1 Sowing in the morning, sowing seeds
 of kindness,   [dewy eve ;
 Sowing in the noon-tide and the
 Waiting for the harvest, and the time
 of reaping,   [the sheaves.
 We shall come, rejoicing, bringing in

CHORUS.

Bringing in the sheaves, bringing in the
 sheaves.   [sheaves ;
We shall come, rejoicing, bringing in the
Bringing in the sheaves, bringing in the
 sheaves,   [sheaves.
We shall come, rejoicing, bringing in the

2 Sowing in the sunshine, sowing in the
 shadows,   [chilling breeze ;
 Fearing neither clouds nor winter's
 By and by the harvest, and the labor
 ended ;   [the sheaves.
 We shall come, rejoicing, bringing in

WHAT A FRIEND.

1 What a friend we have in Jesus,
 All our sins and griefs to bear ;
 What a privilege to carry
 Everything to God in prayer.
 Oh, what peace we often forfeit,
 Oh, what needless pain we bear—
 All because we do not carry
 Everything to God in prayer.

2 Have we trials and temptations?
 Is there trouble anywhere?
 We should never be discouraged,
 Take it to the Lord in prayer.
 Can we find a friend so faithful,
 Who will all our sorrows share?
 Jesus knows our every weakness,
 Take it to the Lord in prayer.

3 Are we weak and heavy-laden,
 Cumbered with a load of care?
 Precious Saviour, still our refuge,—
 Take it to the Lord in prayer.
 Do thy friends despise, forsake thee?
 Take it to the Lord in prayer ;
 In His arms He'll take and shield thee,
 Thou wilt find a solace there.

I LOVE TO TELL THE STORY.

1 I love to tell the Story,
 Of unseen things above,
 Of Jesus and His Glory,
 Of Jesus and His Love !
 I love to tell the Story !
 Because I know it's true ;
 It satisfies my longings
 As nothing else would do.

CHORUS.

I love to tell the Story !
'Twill be my theme in glory,
To tell the Old, Old Story
Of Jesus and His love.

2 I love to tell the Story !
 More wonderful it seems,
 Than all the golden fancies
 Of all our golden dreams.
 I love to tell the Story !
 It did so much for me !
 And that is just the reason,
 I tell it now to thee.

Index

A.

Abide With Me,	143
Ah! My Heart Was Heavy Laden,	83
All Angels Swell a Chorus,	82
Alleluia! Allelulia!	6
Alleluia! Song of Gladness,	164
All's Right, All's Right!	211
And Shall I Turn Back,	105
Angel Voices,	195
A Prayer,	52
Are Thy Burdens Very Heavy,	63
Are We Making the Most of Our Moments,	186
At Midnight Comes the Cry,	121
At the Cross,	133

B.

Battle Song,	190
Battling for the Lord,	112
Bearing the Battle of Jesus,	84
Beautiful City,	95
Beautiful City of God, The,	156
Beautiful Home,	46
Beautiful Sunshine, The,	113
Be Ready for the Call,	124
Be Strong in Jehovah,	183
Bethesda,	184
Birds and Blossoms,	209
Blest Eden,	101
Blessings of the Lord, The,	138
Blessed, Blessed Word of Jesus,	83
Blessed Saviour (Harding),	165
Blessed Saviour (Geibel),	181
Blessed Saviour, Lead Us,	25
Boundless Love,	4
Brightest and Best,	180
Bringing in the Sheaves,	220
Brother Whence Art Thou Steering,	29
But There is a Way,	177

C.

Carry the Message,	16
Children of the Earth Rejoice,	140
Christ Has Come to All,	28
Christian Children Must be Holy,	89
Christian Path, The,	94
Christ is the Conqueror,	54
Christ's Sacrifice,	150
Come Forth,	136
Come Home, Come Home,	13
Come Into the Ark,	81
Come, Thou Almighty King,	111
Come to the Fount,	123
Come Unto Me,	44
Come Unto Me, Ye Weary,	74
Coming Again,	135
Coming Bye and Bye,	178
Consecration,	191
Consider the Lilies,	7
Conquering Ever,	34
Conquer Through the Blood,	148
Conquest and Triumph,	79

D.

Dear Lord We Come to Ask,	67
Depth of Mercy! Can There Be,	163
Dost Thou Care?	80
Drifting,	42

E.

Early Primrose, The,	98
Every Hour I Need Thy Blessing	200

F.

Far Away From the Vale,	46
Farewell,	212
Flight of Time, The,	107
Flower Song,	130
Follow the Master,	12
For Christ's Sake,	73
Forever I'll Be Thine,	51
Forevermore,	126
Forever Thine, Dear Lord,	191
Forward in His Name,	62
Friend of Friends, The,	64

G.

Gentle Shepherd is Our Lord,	199
Gently to Lead Them,	41
Give Your Heart to Jesus,	26
Gloria Patri (Glory Be to the Father),	15
Glory to God in the Highest,	114
Glory to the Cleansing Blood,	31
God the Father Will Forgive You,	123
Growing for Jesus,	188

H.

Happy Children Are We,	97
Happy Land, The	139
Happy Seasons,	66
Hark, Hark, O Hear the Sad Cry,	60
Healing Fountain, A,	102
Hearest Thou Not?	158
Heavenly Father,	39
He is Coming,	157
He Leadeth Me,	218
He Leadeth My Soul,	88
Help Me In,	184
He Planned This Path For Thee,	76
He Slumbers Not,	215
He Who Lived and Loved and Died,	160
Hold My Hand,	198
Holy Father, We Adore Thee,	181
Hosanna Be the Children's Song,	141
Hosanna, Hosanna,	189
How Shall You Stand,	159

I.

I Am Clinging To the Cross,	33
I Am Happy, O So Happy,	32
I Am Resting,	45
I Am the Way,	37
I Cannot Walk Alone,	198
I Have Found a Precious Saviour,	56
I Hear Thy Welcome,	219
I Love to Tell the Story,	220
In Jesus,	162
In My Saviour's Care,	153
In That Day,	86
In the Journey of Life,	8
In the Shadow of the Rock,	72
It Cleanseth Me,	31
I Will Trust,	19

J.

Jerusalem. The Grand,	172
Jesus is Calling the Children,	41
Jesus, Jesus, Blessed Jesus,	63
Jesus! Name of Wondrous Love,	171
Jesus, Our Lord Will Ever Be,	106
Jesus, Our Refuge,	128
Jesus a Little,	11
Just As I Am,	218

L.

Lambs of Jesus,	55
Let Christian Workers Hear the Call,	66
Let Us Wave the Glorious Banner,	112
Lift Heart and Voice,	82
Listen! Listen! He Is Calling,	5
Little Act, A,	96
Little Things,	11
Living for Jesus,	96
Lord is My Shepherd, The,	88
Lord, Remember Me,	115
Lords Prayer, The,	49
Loving Saviour,	52
Loving Words,	59

M.

Make Me Thine,	161
March On, March On,	116
March With Happy Song,	58
Master is Watching, The,	154
May Jesus Christ Be Praised,	3
Mispah,	47
Morning Light, The,	218
My Lord and My God,	160
My Saviour Dwelleth in Heaven,	176
My Soul Be On Thy Guard,	149
My Spirit On Thy Care,	201

O.

Obey His Commands and Do Right	117
O For a Nobler, Brighter Life,	23
O For a Thousand Tongues,	219
O God of Love,	166

Oh How Sweet,	142
O Jesus, My Saviour,	70
O Jesus, Our Jesus,	61
O Let Us Walk,	94
O Lord at Eventide,	35
O Mighty One,	167
One Thing Needful, The,	78
One Thing Thou Lackest,	48
Only Thine, Precious Lord,	161
Onward, Christian Soldiers,	170
O Prodigal Come!	77
O Ring Ye Bells,	27
O the Never Failing Fountain,	102
O the Pure Cleansing Fountain,	192
Out on the Mountain,	13
O Wand'ring Souls Come Near Me,	20

P.

Precious Promise,	219

R.

Rally at the Bugle Call,	116
Rays of Sunshine,	129
Reapers, The,	152
Redemption,	30
Rescue Song,	60

S.

Sabbath Bells,	27
Saved Even Now,	142
Saved, Oh Yes I'm Saved,	30
Saved to Serve,	145
Saviour Onward Lead.	190
Shadow of His Wing, The	90
Shout for Gladness,	210
Shout, Shout With Joy,	135
Shout the Saviour's Praises,	146
Sing More of Heaven,	122
Sing Unto Jesus,	196
Sitting, Resting, Leaning,	132
Some of These Days,	22
Somewhere,	206
Song of Joy, Hope and Trust, A,	125
Song of Love,	110
Song of Spring, A,	216
Sounding His Praises,	40
Stand Up, Stand Up for Jesus,	218
Steadily Advancing,	10
Stream of Light Came In, A,	36
Summer Song, A,	204
Sure Retreat, A,	85
Sweet Hour of Prayer,	219
Sweet Moments,	17
Sweet Name of Jesus,	71
Sweet Old Story, The,	120

T.

Take up the Flag,	99
Temperance Banner,	119
The Long Roll Call is Sounding,	62
Then Away, Away,	75
Then Brother Will You Go,	176
Then Despite Ev'ry Foe,	8
Then March Along,	58
Then Praise to Jesus' Name,	79
There are Days of Silent Sorrow,	108
There is a Bright and Happy Home,	65
There's a Friend We Love,	61
There is Joy,	114
There's Nothing to Fear,	183
They are Covered by the Blood,	68
This is not Your Rest,	177
'Tis With the Righteous Well,	134
To Christ Whose Blood,	70
To Work, To Work!	50
True Shepherd, The,	20
Trusting,	185
Trusting God,	91
Trusting So Sweetly,	103
Trust the Father,	214
'Twas Wondrous Love,	9

W.

Waiting Time, The,	108
Walking by the Saviour's Side,	24
Wave the Royal Banner,	18
We are Traveling Home to Glory,	207
Weber 7's,	163
We Hail Thee Blessed Saviour,	194
We Live to Show,	130
We'll March to War,	100
We Look for a City.	53
We March to Victory,	75
We March With Glad Devotion,	6
We Pass This Way But Once,	89
We're a Happy Band of Workers,	137
We're Going to See the King,	202
We Will go to Sunday School,	209
What a Friend We Have in Jesus,	220
What Are You Doing for Jesus?	14
When His Salvation Bringing,	189
When I Reached the Gates of Glory,	174
When Morning Gilds the Sky,	3
When the Way is so Dark,	57
Who'll be on the Lord's Side?	21
Will the Pearly Gates be Open?	92
Will You be One?	118
Will You Come In?	208
Wise Virgins, The,	121
With Footsteps Firm,	100
Wonderful is the Saviour,	93
Wonderful Saviour, The,	104
Work for All to Do,	38
Working for Jesus,	69
Work for the Night is Coming,	218

Y.

Yield Not to Temptation,	220
Your Influence,	168

www.ingramcontent.com/pod-product-compliance
Lightning Source LLC
Chambersburg PA
CBHW022017220426
43663CB00007B/1112